for

D AIR

"When Scott Mason was a little boy someone must have told him to stop, look and listen. He took those orders to heart. For he sees and hears like few others. And that's what makes him so darn good at telling stories."

–Harry Smith, NBC News Correspondent

"Scott's book is very special! He is quite the wordsmith and stirs my memory of unexplained happenings and very close calls I've personally had in the outdoors... This is a must read."

–Bob Timberlake, Artist

"*Faith and Air* is like a frame that displays verbal photographs of what I love most about North Carolina—the people! Simple. Real. Down-to-earth. Unashamed of faith in God."

–Anne Graham Lotz, Christian Evangelist and Author

"Scott is a gifted writer, and his book of miracles is entertaining, insightful and will inspire every reader."

–The Honorable Jim Hunt, Former Governor, North Carolina

"I am encouraged spiritually by the strength of the stories in *Faith and Air: The Miracle List.*"

–U.S.Congressman Walter Jones, North Carolina

"Scott Mason—given all those stories he has heard—was bound to come up with some stories that take us into other realms. During our weird times of drab certainty, anger, and division, it's refreshing to get into the minds of individual human beings who tell their stories—and to be put there with a writer's humor and bright hope.

–Clyde Edgerton, author of *Papadaddy's Book for New Fathers* and *Walking Across Egypt*

FAITH *and* AIR
the miracle list

FAITH *and* AIR
the miracle list

SCOTT MASON

Light Messages

Durham, NC

Copyright © 2017 Scott Mason

Faith and Air: The Miracle List
Scott Mason
thetarheeltraveler.com
smason@wral.com

First Edition

Published 2017, by Light Messages
lightmessages.com
Durham, NC 27713 USA
SAN: 920-9298

Paperback ISBN: 978-1-61153-225-8
Hardcover ISBN: 978-1-61153-250-0
E-book ISBN: 978-1-61153-224-1
Library of Congress Control Number: 2017941351

I SET OUT TO INTERVIEW people who had supposedly experienced miracles, never realizing how much their miracle stories would affect me. I'm sure they didn't realize it either, but they were preparing me for what I didn't see coming— and in the end, their miracles became one of my own.

–Scott Mason

AUTHOR'S NOTE
Wanderlust

CHARLES KURALT IS MY HERO, even though he died in 1997. Kuralt was a North Carolinian and probably the best television storyteller who ever lived. I was watching TV with my parents one night when one of his *On the Road* stories appeared on the news. When the piece ended I pointed and said, "I wanna do what he does." My folks narrowed their eyes. I wasn't even in the fifth grade yet.

Today, I like to think I'm following Kuralt's path. Though he wandered the country for CBS News, I roam North Carolina for WRAL-TV, profiling the witty and wacky, the talented and inspirational: Artists and authors, musicians and mountaineers, watermen and craftsmen—characters all. How grateful I am for the job that called me to Raleigh, a city where I was born, though not raised, and that's planted me at the powerhouse NBC affiliate.

I'm known as WRAL's Tar Heel Traveler. My stories air Monday through Thursday nights and run about two-and-a-half minutes long, which may seem fleeting, but the stories stay with me. They become part of me. I've told hundreds of Tar Heel Traveler stories, and they don't really blur. I remember each one.

I started in television more than thirty years ago, and my passion for it has never dulled. It's my calling, and I think I knew that even as a kid. I love it because there's always another great story—everywhere there's a story. To paraphrase Kuralt, you don't even have to search very hard; all you have to do is look out the window.

PROLOGUE
Faith and Air

REPORTERS DEAL IN FACTS.

But it's faith that intrigues me, faith I occasionally slip into my TV feature stories that air on the 5:30 p.m. news. And if the station's head honchos are watching, I bet they squirm a bit in their leather chairs, for news and faith are like oil and water, church and state—or church and station. A TV news station tends to get jumpy when it comes to Jesus.

But maybe the honchos aren't watching. It's the 5:30 news after all, and my stories are at the end of the newscast—at 5:55, no less. They're probably slipping into the bathroom so they can be back in their leather chairs for the big show at 6:00 p.m., ready for the lead story, their thoughts on tomorrow's ratings. And so another one of my Tar Heel Traveler stories drifts by—with or without the bosses looking on—delivering, I hope, a two-minute respite from murders and fires and car wrecks.

People tell me their stories, which are like gifts, precious and preserved once I write them and air them on TV. The honchos might be in the restroom, but there's a loyal audience that tunes in—and there's always another great character down the road.

"I died and came back to life."

The man said it as an after-thought. My interview with him was already over, and we stood watching Robert, the Tar Heel Traveler photographer, take down the lights and pack up the gear.

My interview subject was a broadcaster himself, and my story was about his long career and all the famous people he'd met. He'd kept me entertained, but the shocker came with the camera off.

"What?" I said. "You died and came back to life?"

"Oh, that's another story. Some other time," he said and swatted the air.

"No, no," I said. "Tell me."

He at last dug in, talked of floating up to the hospital ceiling, hovering there and looking down, seeing his body stretched on the bed below, dead sure enough. He spoke in a very matter-of-fact manner about watching the nurses cover him with a sheet.

I almost told Robert to yank the camera out again, but we had another story to get to. And what would the honchos say? *Dead, my ass,* they'd say. News doesn't do stories about the unexplained—unless it's Halloween.

But I have managed to steal across the line once in a while. Since the Tar Heel Traveler is a feature series, I can get away with the inspirational to some extent—the spiritual, too. Even so, I did not put together a TV story about the man's experience coming back from the dead. I'd already interviewed him about his radio and TV career.

But after hearing him tell about floating to the ceiling, I did ask if I could call him again and find out more, just for my sake. I was curious.

"Sure," he said and teased me with a few other juicy details—the nurse who spoke up and said, "Let me try," and crawled on top of his corpse and pumped his chest with both hands. "CPR was new back then," he told me. "Hardly anybody had heard of it. Thank God she had."

I began to make a miracle list. The list included a woman who told me she was in a car accident that paralyzed her from the waist down." Doctors said she'd never walk again. She told me the story on Thanksgiving Day while standing on her front porch, ladling bowls of soup to homeless people, making sure the poor had a hot meal.

"Praise the Lord!" the woman whooped to the hungry crowd below. "Praise the Lord!" I bet she belted that refrain a hundred times. I finally jumped in and asked if I could call her sometime and hear more about her miracle story.

"For my own sake," I said. "I'd like to know."

"Amen, brother."

What intrigued me about the people on my miracle list, besides the miracles themselves, was that each had two stories—their miracle story and their other story—and stories with layers are usually the best kinds, like a book with a plot and subplot.

A plane crash survivor near Charlotte made my miracle list. He was a businessman late for his flight one night in 1959 and grabbed the last seat on Piedmont Airlines Flight 349. The plane took off; the man settled back, peered out the window, and thought about opening the book he'd started earlier. He never got the chance. The plane slammed into a mountain—his book still on page thirteen. "My lucky number!" he said.

He was another who told me his story straight on, often sprinkling it with humor. He told me about a bear that came nosing around while he lay on the mountaintop unable to move, his feet twisted in two different directions. The bear crept closer, and the man gathered up his strength and shouted at it, which did the trick. The bear bolted back into the woods. I pictured its tail tucked between its legs if the nubby thing had been long enough.

"What did you say to make him run off?" I asked.

"Git away from me, you ol' furry rascal!"

Details like that made for a compelling story. The vision he had of Jesus wasn't so bad, either.

"Just appeared," he said, "a vision of Jesus, like what you see in a painting. Had a long beard and white robe, and he looks at me and says, 'Be concerned not, I'll be with you always.'"

Two days after the crash, teams found the wreckage, recovered twenty-six bodies, and rescued the flight's only survivor.

"Be concerned not, I'll be with you always," he repeated softly, staring past me out the window.

It was the Pearl Harbor veteran who started me on my collection of miracles, who told me a story so rich and vivid that I thought, *Man, I need to gather these stories.* I felt I needed to collect them because miracles have a tough time making it onto the news. The bosses are skeptical and as a reporter, I suppose I should be, too. But the Pearl Harbor vet and all these other people? I looked into their eyes and saw them remembering and didn't hear them hesitate or trip on a detail or change their story. I believed them and was struck with the notion that what they were telling me was more than just a good story, that it was important. That it needed to be written down.

The miracles gnawed at me. And maybe the man in the white robe did, too. I kept hearing, *I'll be with you always* and felt at times like he was standing a tad too close, poking me with his staff and telling me to get on with it, write the dang things down.

I knew the miracle book would be difficult, phoning all those people, interviewing them again and recording every detail. But the book would be hard for another reason. I knew that in writing about these people I might also discover something about myself, my own faith, and might be thunderstruck by what I'd find. I didn't know, and the not knowing is not exactly inspirational but intimidating. In the end, however, I succumbed and put pen to pad.

There will be skeptics, sure. That's something else that makes this book difficult—proof. I suppose the lack of it is why the honchos don't put faith on air. But I ask them and anyone else who reads the pages that follow to make room for the unexplained. Give the people I profile the benefit of the doubt while suspending your own. To me, their miracle stories are both credible and fascinating, as are their other stories. And stories with layers are the best kind. Amen, brother.

J.D. LANCASTER
Jump

DECEMBER 7, 2004: I was not yet the Tar Heel Traveler in 2004, just a typical reporter stuck in the daily news meeting one December afternoon.

"Got any ideas?" said the ten o'clock producer. She and a dozen other managers stared at me from around an oval table, their eyeballs drilling holes in my head, which was empty of ideas.

The oval table, on the other hand, was a mess, littered with newspapers and pages printed with story checklists. I dabbed a finger on the nearest sheet, twirled it toward me and pretended to look interested. Except, most days the news agenda is like a police blotter you've read a thousand times. Only the names change—and sometimes they don't:

Smith arraignment: 9 a.m.

Jones jury selection: 10 a.m.

I searched for some tantalizing nugget the others had missed, spotted "City Council Meeting: 2 p.m." and pushed the paper away. But those eyeballs hadn't budged.

Mine danced around theirs and landed on the TVs above, a row of three mounted to the wall, and just then a blurry battleship on the middle monitor blew to smithereens, touching off a mushroom cloud that billowed above the wreckage. "Jeez," I muttered. The video was riveting, even in black and white.

"Well," I said, staring at the screen longer than necessary— but that was part of the act: exude casual confidence. "How about Pearl Harbor? It's the anniversary. It's all over CNN." I pulled my eyes from the wreckage and scanned the table. "We could talk to some vets. I got a great contact."

I did have a great contact, a veteran I'd interviewed once for a story about bugle players. The guy's war buddies kept dying, and he took it upon himself to recruit buglers to play Taps at their funerals. I remembered the man as a real go-getter, but then the poor fella had to be. Bugle players were dying, too—there weren't many around anymore. The bugle had become an instrument of the past. And my great contact might have, too.

"Great contact," I repeated to the table. "I'm sure he knows some Pearl Harbor survivors." *But was that guy in World War II?* I couldn't remember.

"What anniversary is it?" It was the ten o'clock producer again, and there was steel in her eyes. "The sixty-third, isn't it?" she said, answering her own question with a question.

Producers, I contend, never get excited about anniversary stories. They like action and they like it now, not five years ago or ten years ago, and for crying out loud, certainly not sixty-three years ago. If they have to have an anniversary story in their newscast, it better be one that ends in a five or zero.

"Yeah, it's the sixty-third," I said. "And we got *great* video of Pearl Harbor." I emphasized "great." Sensationalism sells.

All eyes narrowed, and I could tell the table was mulling the idea. I sucked in a breath and glanced at the overhead clock, which was a tick short of 4:00 p.m. Just six hours till news time, and the ten o'clock show sneaks up fast.

"Look," I said, "why don't I call my guy, see if he knows anyone we can talk to?" The ol' wait-and-see trick—and, hey, maybe that anniversary idea doesn't sound so bad after all.

"Okay," piped the producer, sweeping the air as if swatting a bug. "Go on."

I jumped from my seat and scampered for the door—in news, you learn to exude purpose by doing everything fast. And dear God, you better exude purpose when you can't even remember the name of your great contact.

Just before exiting I threw another glance at CNN where thick black smoke billowed from the screen. The crumpled battleship was sinking.

*

I like a good story, fact or fiction—the more melodramatic, the better.

In eighth grade, I wrote a paper on Leopold and Loeb, wealthy and brilliant law students from Chicago who in 1924 set out to commit the perfect crime. They picked a neighborhood kid at random, offered him a ride, and cracked him on the head with a chisel. Bobby was fourteen-years-old and dead before his killers poured hydrochloric acid on his face. They left his body in a culvert, drove off, and went about their days like nothing happened. But it wasn't long before the perfect crime began unraveling like a frayed rope—in fact, *Rope* is the name of the movie about the crime.

I threw myself into the research and even more into the writing. No way was I going to hand my Social Studies teacher a ten-page snoozer paraphrased from the *Encyclopedia Britannica*. I'd pizzazz her with a thirty-page novella that wouldn't let her sleep at night.

Except she didn't look the least bit baggy-eyed the day she handed back my masterpiece. I'd bound it in a plastic sheath with a bold title page: IMPERFECT MURDER!

I flipped to the back and discovered a red A, which I was happy about, of course, but that's all she'd written. I fanned the other pages to make sure and found nothing but white space in the margins.

What I'd been looking for was something as flashy and bold as my title, something like: *Blockbuster! Kept me turning pages into the wee, wee hours!* I longed for a best-seller endorsement, and my eighth-grade mind told me I'd have to try harder next time.

The next time was in high school when I penned a forty-pager on Joe McCarthy's reckless accusations of Communism. I waited for my teacher's reaction to my blow-by-blow account, but when he thumped it on my desk, a black D glared at me from the front page. The only consolation was that he had at least included a comment, scrawled across the bottom in bold ink: *Melodrama went out years ago!*

*

I marched through the newsroom, into the afternoon melee that only grows louder as news time creeps closer. Phones ring, scanners squawk, producers scream. "No way! My lead story just crashed and burned!"

I escaped to the sanctuary of my cubicle, plopped in my chair, and felt all my fake confidence run out of me like ink from a gnawed pen. But the clock still ticked. It read 4:08 in the bottom corner of my computer screen.

I rolled forward, clicked on "News Archive," typed *Bugle* and *Taps,* hit Enter, and just like that, my old story flashed up. I almost planted a smooch on the screen, no matter the dust.

I started reading and found the name of my great contact— *Yes!*—who was a veteran of the—*Korean War? Oh, don't tell me.* But it did tell me; it told me my World War II idea was up in flames. I pushed my chair away, leaned back, and sighed and for the first time noticed the swirly brown stain on the ceiling tile above my head.

Coffee. I need coffee.

It was the best cup I never had. I'd just rounded my cubicle corner when the six o'clock producer called out and waved me to his desk. He was young and hip with slicked-back hair and a thing for tight, bright soccer shirts. He was also known for surfing the Web for factoids he could slip into his show.

"You're doing Pearl Harbor, aren't you?" he said, his eyes locked on his laptop.

"Well…"

"Look at this," he said, pointing to a full page of type, too long to read quickly. "It's the *Arizona.* One of the survivors is in Johnston County." He scrolled down and… "That's him." He tapped the name: *J.D. Lancaster.*

"The *Arizona,*" he repeated. "Man, if you could find him…" He didn't finish his sentence, but the way he said it made me think there probably weren't too many *Arizona* survivors around. The producer was half my age, but all those factoids must have lodged in his head. I'd have to brush up on my history and track down Lancaster. And quick.

*

I found his phone number on the Internet. J.D. Lancaster lived in the little town of Pine Level, but I felt sure I wouldn't reach him even as I punched the numbers on my cell. Reporters are naturally skeptical.

"Helloo?" answered a woman on the second ring. I was surprised someone had answered at all, and when she told me to hold on a minute after I asked for Mr. Lancaster, I tightened my grip on the phone. I was also surprised he was alive.

"This is J.D.," came the voice, loud and strong. Mine was halting.

"Mr. Lancaster," I muttered and sat up straight. I explained who I was and why I'd called. "Understand you were on the *Arizona*?"

"Yes, sir!" he said and jumped into his story. Sixty-three years and he talked like it was fresh.

I interrupted to tell him we wanted to come to his house with a camera. "In an hour," I said, squeezing the phone. People like to be prepared for an interview. They need time—something TV crews never have enough of. But J.D. didn't hesitate.

"It's the brick duplex behind the brick houses past the gas station. There's a pecan tree in the front yard and an old blue Buick in the drive."

I scratched the directions on my pad, thanked him, hung up, and leaned back. *Whew*, I thought and again noticed the soiled ceiling tile—the Big Dipper above my head. The stars had aligned.

I'd grab a coffee for the road.

*

I rode with photographer Ken Corn, and with a name like Corn, we in the newsroom naturally called him "the Kernel," though I'm sure he preferred *Colonel*. Kernel Ken sported a military crew cut but was a beefy sort with a belly laugh, who often entertained me with rambunctious tales of his high school days. He reminded me of a TV version of Van Gogh, a kind of restless, misunderstood artist. The Kernel dreamed of producing grand, life-changing documentaries but instead found himself slapping together fleeting news stories lucky to run ninety seconds. His reward was a late shift, fast food, and tension at home for rarely seeing his wife and kid. Good thing he had that hearty laugh. He'd throw back his head and spew out his pent-up frustration— though whatever artistic talent he possessed remained buried beneath the blubber of daily news.

We pulled up to the brick duplex with the pecan tree and parked behind the blue Buick. I stood by while Ken unloaded his camera gear from the trunk, and a moment later I heard the storm door rattle and caught my first sight of J.D. Lancaster. He stood on his front stoop, was around five-foot-seven, trim, and wore a black bow tie and sleek silver windbreaker. He looked dapper, I thought. His warm smile stretched the lines of his long face. "Mr. Lancaster?" I said. He looked too good to be true.

"You got him!"

7

Ken and I clunked through the storm door, hauling tripod, camera, and light kit, and dropped it all in his cramped living room. His wife peeked in from the hallway, no doubt alarmed by all the heavy thumping. She had a nervous smile and began moving trinkets around on an end table, and when she finally stopped and studied her work, I thought she might start rearranging again. Instead, she backed away and disappeared down the hall.

"Have a seat," J.D. said, gesturing to the couch. On the wall above it hung a large framed photo of a battleship, long and gray and loaded with lots of steel. Its guns pointed fore and aft, and stars and stripes flew from bow and stern.

"The *Arizona*?" I asked.

"That's it," he said and jumped in where he'd left off on the phone. "I'll never forget it, never..."

It was exactly what I didn't want: for him to spill his best sound before the camera rolled. I cut him off mid-stream and shot a glance at Ken who'd set up one of the lights.

Ken was good with lights and knew how to create a colorful hue, but at that point, the only hue was on his face, which was beet red. The Kernel was slinging around extension cords as though bent on whipping the assignment editor who'd stuck him on the night shift.

"I've relived it no telling how many times," J.D. said moments later. "They looked like crows," he said of the Japanese planes swooping in that Sunday morning. And so began his story of Pearl Harbor—with the camera rolling at last.

"Boom, boom, boom, boom. Everything went up. Boom," he said, flitting his hands. A bomb had ripped through the ship, igniting the ammunition magazine. "I was about ten feet from where it hit, and guys were lying all over everywhere. I would see someone and grab their hand, but when I grabbed it, their skin would come right off." I winced and wondered whether that would make the cut, but Ken kept right on rolling.

"I remember waking up in the water, and the water was on fire, and I had to keep dunking under to keep from being burned. There were so many explosions going off it was like the water was bouncing. Men were screaming all around me."

He peered at me then, his thin face like chiseled stone. J.D. was eight-five—twenty-two at the time of the attack—and one of about 300 to survive the *Arizona* out of 1400 on board. He was the only survivor from North Carolina.

In just minutes, that huge 600-foot battleship slipped beneath the flaming waters of Pearl Harbor, taking with it more than 1000 dead crewmen and entombing them inside its sunken hull. After the sinking, J.D. helped recover bodies. "We had to go underwater with no light and feel around with our arms up. If a body was down there it would be floating on the ceiling because of the air in the stomach. Sometimes you'd get a pillow and think it was one. It was spooky. When we found a body we grabbed hold and punctured it with a knife to let out the air, and that way we could put the body under our arms and carry it. I guess we got right many that way."

I drew back and grimaced. "Gosh," I said, "how were you able to…"

"Cigarettes," he said.

"Cigarettes?"

He explained that cigarettes were kept in airtight tins and that dive teams hunted for those, too. "When you would come up they didn't ask if you found a dead body. They wanted to know if you found any cigarettes."

I stole another look at Ken who was bent to the viewfinder. I worried about making slot at 10 p.m. but wasn't about to tell the Kernel to stop rolling, not with J.D. embroiled in his story—which triggered another story.

He talked about a landing ship he'd been assigned to after Pearl Harbor. "Took a torpedo during the night and the ship was cut in half, and I jumped in the water with no life preserver." He said he clung to a life raft, helpless to aid anyone still on board; all he could do was listen to the horrifying screams in the dark. "Then it got completely quiet, and you knew everyone else had drowned."

According to J.D., the ship had 700 crewmen and just forty-five lived, and today he was the only one left. "The only one," he said.

"Do you ever wonder *why* you survived?" I asked.

"'Cause the Lord had something else for me to do." He thumped his fist on the La-Z-Boy armrest. "God wants me to tell this. Keep telling it, keep telling it," he said and thumped, and I knew that's how I'd end my news story, with that sound bite and fist thump.

Except the story wasn't over. He told me that before the landing ship went down he stood on the deck bleeding from his ears with nothing but blackness in front of him and a voice in his head. It was God's voice, he said, telling him to jump into the darkness, into that wide-open sea. He didn't want to jump, couldn't see anything in front of him, but the voice was clear. He was convinced it was God, and so he obeyed and hit the water, and a moment later the inflatable raft drifted up to him out of nowhere.

He stared at me hard, eyes fixed on mine. "A miracle," he whispered, and a little shiver crawled up my spine, and I looked away; the moment seemed too intense. I turned toward Ken—who was *not* rolling.

Perhaps by then TV news had sliced the Van-Gogh right out of him. It's instinctive—news people generally grow squirrely at the mention of God. Faith doesn't fit on air. Miracles are not news. The Kernel had powered down the camera.

But J.D. kept talking, and I kept listening. He told me about catching pneumonia years after the war, lying in a hospital bed, near death with no hope; the doctor had given up. And then a bird appeared at his window. "A bird," he said, "and it perched on the windowsill and looked at me. That was the sign I'd been praying for, and I knew I'd be all right, and I was. The doctor couldn't believe it."

J.D. held my gaze, and another moment passed between us. This time I did not turn away. "Can I interview you again?" I asked before I knew I had and heard a jumble of lights clatter behind me. I'm sure Ken had thrown up his hands, thinking I was nuts, thinking he had to re-set the gear for round two. "Not interview you now," I quickly told J.D., "but sometime later. Without the camera."

"Yes," he said and gripped my arm, his eyes huge behind his glasses. "Keep telling it, keep telling it," he said, and squeezed.

"I'll try," I said, or more like muttered. My response sounded limp in comparison to his plea.

"Keep telling it."

I would do what I could in a minute and a half on the ten o'clock news, but I felt J.D. deserved more, and I wanted more, too. I wanted to know about that bird, implausible as it seemed.

News had infused me with cynicism, but another part of me remained fascinated by the unexplained. In a way, I felt I was also standing on a ledge, peering into darkness, news holding me fast to solid ground, and yet I wanted to believe God was out there somewhere, that life wasn't just some black hole devoid of miracles. But did I have the faith to make that jump?

I clunked out J.D.'s door, telling him I'd call sometime, telling myself I'd be back, promising myself one day I'd be back.

*

December 8, 2005:

It took me twelve months and a day.

I thought of J.D. often during that long stretch, thought I better go interview him before it's too late—I cringed every time I turned to the obituaries. The reporter in me kept urging me to pick up where I'd left off, write a magazine article, make some money. Why not?

But in truth, I had no interest in writing a magazine article. What I really wanted was to satisfy my curiosity and fulfill my obligation. That's what it was: an obligation. J.D. had planted a seed in me, and I felt I owed it to him—and Him—to see what I could do to nurture it. I felt I had to go back. For God's sake, I had to.

It's just that I wasn't sure I had the talent to tell J.D.'s story. It would mean interviewing him at length, writing down quotes—could I write that fast?—gathering all those nitty-gritty details: *What was the day like? What were you wearing? What were you thinking? What happened when...?* Time and again I shook off the idea of returning: *Can't. Not gonna do it. But maybe I should try. If only I had the time...*

Time came by way of Divine Intervention—if there is such a thing. An official notice arrived in the mail, stamped with a seal. I wondered at first if I'd broken some law and opened it gingerly, afraid of tearing the envelope. I slipped out the document and read the bold type.

This is a summons for jury duty, it began, and I read the rest with growing interest. I'd never been called for jury duty before. Maybe I'd get to hear a big murder case.

Report at 9 a.m. December 8th, the summons stated, and I knew the TV station would have no choice but to allow me the time off. It would be a welcome break from the daily grind even if it meant sitting in a courthouse all day—or maybe weeks if it *was* a big case. My heart started thumping, and then my eyes landed on the small print at the bottom of the page: *Please call the courthouse the day prior to your scheduled appointment to confirm you are needed.*

I called on December 7th, Pearl Harbor Day, and the recording told me I was not needed for jury duty. *Too bad,* I thought. Now I'd have to tell the station I didn't need the time off. *Or maybe...*

The realization hit me. Here was my chance, right now, tomorrow. My heart started pounding again, both out of excitement and fear. The old doubts returned, whether I had the talent to complete what I'd begun. But I also felt it was more than mere coincidence my opportunity had arrived on Pearl Harbor Day, and that feeling of fate is what ultimately pushed me over the edge. The time had come for me to take the jump.

*

Pine Level is a forty-five-minute drive from Raleigh. I drove with the radio off and thought of all the questions I'd ask J.D. and shook my head at the irony: I was going to visit a man of God by way of deception. The station thought I was in court, and I should have been pleased with my charade but instead gripped the wheel when I turned onto J.D.'s road. The sign read CHURCH STREET.

I rolled into the drive, half expecting J.D. to swing open the storm door, smile, and windmill his arm at me. I had called to let him know I was coming, but the duplex was quiet, the blinds shut, and I told myself it wasn't too late to back out. Maybe he wasn't home; I didn't see the blue Buick, but I did notice an American flag flying in his front yard and scooted closer to the windshield and squinted. I'd read newspaper clippings that mentioned J.D. hoisting the stars and stripes every morning, just like someone had each day at the *Arizona* Memorial in Pearl Harbor. The flag flapped and the winter sun winked, and I think that's what finally got me, the image I had in my mind of J.D. raising Old Glory. I'm sure he probably saluted; in fact, so did I before pushing open the car door.

I've seen my share of tragedy as a reporter. I've covered the deaths of sons and daughters and knocked on the doors of their mothers and fathers. J.R. Moehringer once said, "As a newspaper writer, you spend much of your time walking up dirty steps to talk to dirty people about dirty things. Then, once in a great while, you meet an antidote to all that dirt."

The reporter, I think, is both sympathizer and scavenger, feeding off tragedy but affected by it, too, for writing about it might help prevent other tragedies. The typical reporter wants to change the world—and sell newspapers and boost ratings. He's both sneaky and sincere; the truth hovers somewhere over the threshold.

But once in a while there's an antidote to all that, someone on the other side of the door whose story is greater than the reporter's own ego, someone whose story is not just a story but something bigger, worth more than columns in a paper or a slot on a newscast.

That's the way I felt walking up J.D.'s front steps, clutching my little notepad. I was there both as a reporter and not as a reporter—my identity hovered somewhere in between. I see it now as my axis, my turning point, when something in me began to shift from reporter to writer. I'd come, not just to document one man's harrowing experience on earth, but to delve into some deeper mystery beyond. And I hoped I had it in me to do it.

His wife opened the door when I knocked. Her hair was gray and her face expressionless. She simply swung the door wide and ushered me in as though she'd been expecting me. But I'm not sure J.D. had.

He was in his favorite chair, but he was not the man I'd seen the year before. "Hi ya," he said, and I was about to tell him not to get up when I realized he probably couldn't anyway. He was hooked to an oxygen tank with tubes sticking out of his nose. His condition shouldn't have surprised me—I had read about his damaged lungs, still scarred all these years after Pearl Harbor. But I'd also read about him performing in a Baptist quartet with his three brothers. J.D. had soldiered on. He threw me a smile, and his eyes brightened behind his oversized glasses.

"Sittdown, sittdown," he said, and waved at the couch. His voice sounded strong, but his body looked frail, and his clothes seemed to illustrate the contrast. He wore a red pajama top with gray flannel slacks, as though he'd forgotten to get all the way dressed.

His wife poked at the couch cushions, trying to fluff them. I sat, and J.D. and I exchanged "How-you-doin's," and then we both turned and looked at her, the third party in the room. She finally folded her hands, excused herself and disappeared down the hall.

It felt funny not being under deadline. I had the whole day to interview J.D. and months or years or however long it took to write his story—if I wrote it at all. I should have been at ease plunked in the cushions of his couch with a great day ahead of me. Nobody even knew where I was, only J.D. and his wife—and maybe the lady at Bojangles' just across the county line who'd served me coffee and a biscuit. "Whatchya reportin' on today?" she'd asked, recognizing me from the news.

"Oh, nothin' much," I drawled.

"Ohhhh," she said with a wiggle and a grin, as if I was on some undercover assignment, which I suppose I was. "Well, I'll be watchin'," she said, and winked.

I should have felt perfectly satisfied, but I was antsy in J.D.'s living room. Maybe it was seeing him in his pajama top and the tubes running from his nose. I felt I had to interview him right now, scribble down every detail as best I could, because this might be my only chance.

"Born November 6th, 1919," he said. I'd asked him to start at the beginning. "Born on Buffalo Road between Smithfield and Selma in a house with a green top. My father was a minister and farmer. Had ten or fifteen acres of cotton, and it struck me all of a sudden: *I'm not gonna have nothing. Why don't I just go do something about it?* So I slung that bag of cotton up on the porch. I said, 'Yeah, I think I picked my last bag. Think I'll join the Navy 'cause there's nothing here for me.'"

It was 1939, and J.D. hitchhiked to Raleigh to sign up, then reported to boot camp in Norfolk, Virginia. "I'd never seen the ocean till then. 'Whoo, what have I done?' I just looked and looked and said, 'What have I got into?'"

The Navy eventually packed him onto a freight train with other recruits and shipped him to California. "What a ride that was," he said. "Never been so smutty; all that coal. You was just as black as smoke when you got there."

He arrived in San Pedro and took his first step aboard the battleship USS *Arizona*. "We got out of dry dock," he said, "and that's when we headed for Pearl Harbor. That was our home base.

"I was assigned to a five-inch broadside gun. It came out of the turret, the barrel did, and that's where we stayed, in the turret, that's where we slept. So at night if something happened, you didn't have to run to your gun. You were already at your gun."

J.D. was good at painting a picture. I could see him holed up in his little compartment with his bedroll, jumping for his weapon at the slightest sound, wearing only his skivvies.

He was a Seaman First Class, and his starting pay was thirty-six dollars a month. "We'd pool our money and go ashore, go to the canteen, lay our money in the middle of the table and drink and have a good time. Can of beer was five or ten cents." I pictured him, rosy faced and thin as a post, kicking back in a chair, tilting his beer and wearing a huge grin. "We had to think of things to amuse us, to break the monotony."

He was at Pearl Harbor more than a year before the bombing. "I had a feeling something was going to happen," he said, recalling the night of December 6th. "We were too relaxed, too much partying, too many men going ashore. Half our crew was out that night, drunk on the island."

He'd been assigned to operate the captain's private boat, and as J.D. waited to ferry guests back to port that night he chatted with a few of his crewmates and told them he was convinced an attack was coming. "We're sitting ducks," he said. But one of the men scoffed at the idea, arguing that no enemy in their right mind would take that chance, not with all the Allied planes patrolling the ocean. They went at it so loudly an orderly stormed out of the captain's quarters and snapped at them to pipe down.

Tension was high. In fact, I could feel it now in J.D.'s living room, a world away from the *Arizona* and two-thirds of a century after the attack. But the attack was imminent. J.D. leaned forward and folded his hands, and I gripped my pen. "We'd just finished breakfast when the first Japanese plane flew over Ford Island. I was polishing the captain's boat, and I heard a lot of noise, and I looked up and saw the planes coming right at us. I saw those rising suns under the wings, and I knew what was coming."

I knew what he meant by the rising suns—the Japanese symbol.

"I'd never seen so many planes, and I said, 'Boys, remember what I was telling you? It's happening.'" Those were the boys he'd been arguing with the night before. He never saw them again.

J.D. and I were face to face, and his was grave, but he spoke evenly, deliberately, not loud or soft, just straight on, which somehow made his account even more compelling.

"That first plane, I could see the pilot, his teeth shining, could almost see the color of his eyes he was so close."

I could see it, too, even as my pen raced across the page. I knew some of my words were so slanted they'd be almost impossible to read, but I didn't dare go back and fix them now. It didn't seem important to read my writing then. It was better to see the planes.

"It was like a nightmare. Everything happening, the popping of guns, explosions in the water. My battle station was way up forward, and I was running."

A hundred feet before he reached his post, the *Arizona* took a powerful blow. "I mean we took a hit. Five-hundred tons of powder went off—you know that was a big bomb— and that blew the ship all to pieces. If I had got to my battle station it would've been right on top of me, would have killed me." Instead, it blew J.D. off his feet and into the burning sea.

"All I remember is waking up in the water, and the water was on fire. My hair had burned off, and I had bruises and cuts all over my arms and legs. I looked up and saw men burned black piling out of the hatches and falling over the deck. I did the first thing that popped in my mind. I tried to get back to the ship."

He swam about 400 feet to the captain's private boat, which was tied to the *Arizona's* stern. By the time he reached it, the battleship had already sunk at least six feet. "Nothing but twisted metal."

He looped a rope around the ship's rail and climbed on board. "And there were guys laying everywhere, burnt completely black." He dragged as many men as he could to the captain's boat, powered the engine and sped for the beach just a few hundred yards away. Then he turned around and did it again till the people on the beach told him to stop. Too dangerous, they said. "'The ones over there, they aren't gonna survive anyway,' they told me. In fact, not a one of them survived that I brought back. Not a one."

He stared at the floor a moment before continuing. "All my clothes were burnt off. Had nothing but my underwear, and a lady gave me a pair of civilian pants and a necktie. The necktie I used as a belt to hold my britches up."

The next time he boarded the captain's boat was to help pick up bodies floating in the water. "We'd tie them together, sometimes have eight of them dragging behind the boat, and we'd drag them to the beach and go after more."

J.D. broke off his story, reached for a crinkled magazine on the coffee table, and flipped to the place he wanted—or rather, the magazine landed there on its own, as if its worn crease had memorized the section. J.D. pointed to the dramatic two-page spread: A picture of the battered *Arizona*, smoke billowing from one page to the next.

"I never will forget. I stood and looked, and what I saw was this, and I knew in my heart that someday we'd get even with them. And then I asked the Lord to forgive me for having those thoughts, those evil thoughts against them."

It was the first time since I'd arrived that he had mentioned the Lord, which is what I had come for in the first place, to hear his miracle stories. And yet I figured his Pearl Harbor story was somehow part of the whole, that without it the miracles he experienced later might not have the same meaning.

Re-telling Pearl Harbor had energized J.D., and I wondered a moment who needed the oxygen tank more—him or me. I wrung out my wrist and wrote down the rest.

He told me about the injuries he suffered in the attack and not just his lungs. He also lost part of his hearing but kept on anyway. With the *Arizona* destroyed, he boarded another battleship, the *West Virginia*, and spent the next six days volunteering for whatever needed to be done. The Navy, meanwhile, didn't know what had happened to him and sent his family back home a sobering telegram:

YOUR SON JAMES DANIEL LANCASTER SEAMAN FIRST CLASS US NAVY IS MISSING FOLLOWING ACTION IN THE PERFORMANCE OF HIS DUTY IN THE SERVICE OF HIS COUNTRY.

His family braced for the worst—except for J. D.'s father who refused to give in to grief and instead urged faith. "My father's prayers," J.D. said, "that's what brought me through. The almighty Lord was lookin' after me."

Three weeks after the first telegram, the Navy sent a second one:

THE NAVY DEPARTMENT IS GLAD TO INFORM YOU THAT YOUR SON JAMES DANIEL LANCASTER SEAMAN FIRST CLASS US NAVY PREVIOUSLY REPORTED MISSING FOLLOWING ACTION IN THE PERFORMANCE OF HIS DUTY IS NOW REPORTED TO BE A SURVIVOR…THE ANXIETY CAUSED YOU BY THE PREVIOUS MESSAGE IS DEEPLY REGRETTED.

"I was assigned to another ship at Guadalcanal in the South Pacific. A lot of those islands needed some reinforcements, and that was my job, taking troops to those islands. But one day they called me and said, 'We got a job for you, and it ain't gonna be easy.'"

I couldn't help the smile tugging at my mouth, brought on by J.D.'s down-home lingo in the midst of all the drama.

When he learned of orders to send his ship to the island of Munda, J.D. confronted his superior.

"I said to the captain, 'Where's our escort?' The captain shook his head and said, 'We don't have any. We're gonna try to slip in.' I said, 'This sounds like a suicide mission.' He just turned his head and walked away, and I said, 'Lord, have mercy.'"

LST-342 was not exactly a push over. It was more than 300 feet long and weighed 1600 tons—I researched it later.

"We got out to sea with the moon shining bright. As bright as a searchlight. "But later on the moon went down, and it got dark." And so the crew slept. It was the night of July 18, 1943. "I went below and lied down on the bare deck underneath the ladder and used a life preserver as a pillow. That's all I had."

He stretched out in the ship's bow, while most of the crew bunked in the stern. "Something inside me knew," he said. "I was just lying there, waiting for it to happen."

I waited, too—for J.D. to deliver the blow and describe the catastrophe that surely was bound for the sleeping ship. But he never even heard the explosion.

"I don't know how long I was unconscious. I lay on the deck bleeding, blood coming out of my mouth, my ears."

A Japanese torpedo had sliced the boat in two. The stern began sinking immediately as J.D. raced to the upper deck.

"I saw two guys with packs on their backs. I said, 'Don't jump in with those packs on. You'll drown.' They took them off and jumped over, and I never saw them again. They drowned, I know they did. There was nobody there to pick them up."

I watched him swallow hard, and when he began again his voice was softer, almost a whisper. "I was standing there looking," he said, addressing the wall rather than me. Maybe it was just his oversized glasses that exaggerated his gaze, but I don't think so. I think he was seeing it again in his mind, right there in his living room all these years later—except what he saw was nothing.

"I was on the bow, and it was pitch-black, and that voice said, 'Jump over, J.D.' It was just as plain as if you were standing next to me, but there wasn't nobody beside me. That was the voice of Jesus directing me. I knew who it was, nobody but the Lord. So he was testing me; he was testing my faith."

It occurred to me that J.D. was testing mine. His testimony was riveting, but… I couldn't help it, the reporter in me couldn't help it—I was hearing a voice, too, the whisper of doubt, no doubt about it, and how disappointing it was. Or maybe I was disappointed in myself. I wanted so much to believe J.D., but all I had was his account and nobody to back him up—except maybe Jesus and He wasn't talking, not to me at least.

"I couldn't see nothing," J.D. said. "I was out there by myself. The whole other part of the ship had gone down; it was under. If I jump, there's nobody there to pick me up. I don't even know if I can swim."

I watched him bow his head and stare at his shoes. "It takes something strong…," he said, without finishing the thought. He didn't need to. I pictured him holding fast to the deck rail, that vast dark sea in front of him, and wondered what I would have done.

"You concentrate," he said. "You think. You recognize that voice. That voice is different than any other voice. I knew who it was."

He looked up, and I saw puddles in his eyes and knew what was coming next but flinched just the same when he said it.

"I jumped."

Neither of us spoke for half a minute.

"I jumped in the water with no life preserver," he said at last, "and I realized I couldn't swim with my coveralls on. So

I laid on my back and got to wiggling and kicking, and those coveralls went right off, and I said, 'Let's see if I can swim.'"

He swam just a short way before he spotted the lifeboat.

"'Seven-hundred men have just given their lives and there's an empty raft out here floating, just waiting for J.D.' That's what was in my mind. I said, 'Well, I know you had the thing planned out, Lord. I'm trying to carry out your plan.' So I got in the raft, and I'd stopped bleeding then. I stayed in that raft, and I said, 'Where are all those guys on the ship? Surely I'm not the only one.' So I got to hollering."

Three men in the water heard him call out and swam to the raft, and they all sat listening to the cries from the sinking ship. "You never heard such an awful fuss. Then it got completely quiet, and you knew then everyone else had drowned."

The rest of that day, the four of them drifted in enemy waters.

"I said, 'I heard the Japs don't pick up no survivors. If they come along and see us they'll use us for target practice.' I told them, 'I'm gonna get off the raft and hold on and just keep my eyes above water.'"

At dusk, they spotted a distant boat gunning straight for them.

"You never had your heart beat any harder than when you don't know what it is coming at you," he said and thumped the La-Z-Boy armrest. "We got in the water, and my heart was pounding and pounding."

The men peeped over the raft, straining to see if the approaching boat was friend or foe. "After all I'd been through

I wasn't going to get shot or be taken prisoner." As the boat closed in, he thought of drowning himself.

But then it made a slight turn, and there was Old Glory fluttering on a pole. "I see it, and there it was, the most beautiful flag I'd ever seen, and when you look through tears..." He choked up, trembling in his easy chair. I held my pen to my pad, waiting for the rest because I knew this was a pivotal moment—two moments, really, the one then and the one now in his living room.

"We saw that flag flying on the mast." He was crying even as he told me, but smiling, too. "She looks different through tears, but that was the prettiest sight I ever seen. Boy, that thing was beautiful. We saw the American flag and cried like babies."

It was a small Navy boat that drew alongside the raft, and its crew reached out and pulled the men on board. Once below deck, somebody handed J.D. a small bottle.

"You know what it was? Four-star Brandy. I can see it now. Had those little metal caps on it, but I drank it all. About choked me to death, but I drank every bit, and I remember hearing that bottle crash on the deck." He'd fallen asleep holding it.

J.D. grinned at me, and I smiled at his bright eyes, dancing behind his oversized glasses. "That was the last thing I remember," he said.

*

J.D.'s wife came in to check on him, probably tired of having to hole herself up in the back bedroom. She leaned down and touched his hand, and I pretended to busy myself with my notes.

I flipped through the pages and re-wrote some of my chicken scratch so I'd be able to transcribe it later. I was new to this kind of reporting. In TV the camera is my note taker, my notepad little more than a prop. A single pad can last me months.

I knew I had a good war story, but I'd come for the miracles. Was it a miracle J.D. had survived two dramatic ship sinkings or just good drama with a bit of the Lord thrown in? Or maybe dumb luck?

I turned to a new sheet and thought I heard a sigh from J.D.'s wife before she turned for the hall again. *Sorry*, I wanted to tell her, but she was already gone.

J.D. also watched her go and told me he'd met his wife in California—but not *that* wife. The revelation surprised me. I didn't realize he'd been married twice.

"She's my third wife," he said, pointing to the hall.

Thrice? I thought. The man was full of revelations.

He told me about the plane crash he survived a few weeks after being plucked from the sea. He was flying from Seattle to San Diego, just J.D. and the pilot in a small plane when the engine suddenly died, forcing them to bail. "I froze at the door and he had to kick me out," J.D. said. It was the first time he'd ever jumped from a plane, and when he did a strong wind snatched his parachute and dragged him over cactus bushes in the California desert. "Tore me to pieces. Some guys saw me and got me to the hospital. I had Band-Aids all over."

He told me of the months he spent at the naval hospital in San Diego. He was racked with injuries from the plane crash, the LST sinking, and *Arizona* bombing—thrice was right. Even now, he said, he can't taste or smell anything.

His future brother-in-law owned a plumbing business in San Diego and when J.D. was finally well, his in-law taught him the trade. Eventually, J.D. moved home to Johnston County. It was 1948, and he and his wife settled in Smithfield where he opened a plumbing business of his own. I had read that J.D. was a great plumber. "A feisty guy," his nephew once told the local paper. "Time was money, and he was fast about getting around."

I had also read about another nephew, a golfer, and that J.D. had built him a putter out of pieces of iron and rebar. That nephew was Neal Lancaster who went on to become a PGA Tour Professional. J.D. was apparently a resourceful guy, too.

A short time after moving to Smithfield, J.D. and his wife adopted a child. He told me the story with as much intensity as he had talked of Pearl Harbor and the landing ship. I should have asked why they adopted in the first place, but he was thumping the armrest again. "We went to Hillsborough, and I said, 'Lord, give me the right child for me and my wife.' And they brought out this child, and she took my finger and wouldn't turn me a loose."

The child was a two-and-a-half-month-old baby girl.

"Every time I looked down she was staring me in the eyes. Even the nurse saw it and says, 'This is the child for you.'"

It was another good story, a nugget that seemed important— along with the postscript: "Me and my wife smoked, but after that day we never smoked again, not another cigarette. That cured us."

He skipped ahead and talked of his father, the Reverend Lancaster. It was the reverend who had refused to believe his son was dead after the attack at Pearl Harbor and who had later faced death himself. J.D. said his father asked God for a sign, and God sent him one—a dove that landed on the windowsill of his hospital room. "Walked on the ledge of the window," J.D. said "The dove looked right straight at him." Reverend Lancaster was due to have his gallbladder removed the next morning. "And when they came to get him he said, 'You don't have to take me. The Lord has cured me. He sent me a messenger, and the message is you can send me home. I'm gonna be all right.'" J.D. laughed. "My daddy died twenty-four years later with that gallbladder still in him."

J.D. told me about his own hospital stay, the time he had pneumonia and was near death. "And while I was there I thought about my daddy. I said to the Lord, 'You sent a messenger to my daddy and told him he was healed.' I said, 'I'm gonna watch that window as long as I'm here.'

"My children came to see me, and they brought my granddaughter, and I was looking for the messenger at my window. And while they were there, here came this little bird. He was white and perched on the sill outside the window and kept walking back and forth, and my granddaughter kept raising her hands, trying to catch him, and he came down to me; my head was near the window, and he looked at me. He's looking through the window, seeing if he could see me. That's what he was doing, 'cause when he seen me he stopped. And I said, 'Ah, ha!' I said, 'You can go now. I've got the message,' and he turned, and off he went. And my children said, 'Daddy, what's going on?' I said, 'Me and the Lord, we got something between us. He gave me a message. I'm going home.' And the doctor sent me home that same day."

I wrote it all down but did so feeling as if my news director was peering over my shoulder, nudging me to record the names of the children, the doctor's name and nurses. He'd want corroborating witnesses, hard evidence. All I really had was J.D.'s word.

He told me about surviving other serious bouts of pneumonia and facing death many times. One day, he said his doctor called and asked him to come in.

"I said, 'Doc, what's up?' He said, 'Nothing. I just want to talk to you.' He said, 'I've looked at all your records, and I just want to tell you what's come to my mind.' He said, 'You are a miracle person. It's unbelievable to have the emphysema like you have and survive. To have pneumonia five times and survive... It would blow the mind of every doctor. I think the Lord has something else for you to do.'"

I imagined the old physician in a cardigan sweater, hands folded on a heavy mahogany desk and J.D. looking the way he looked now, wearing that delicious grin, eyes bright and dancing.

I found I envied J.D., and the irony of our meeting was not lost on me—me, the reporter questioning a man of faith. We brought two different perspectives to the dimly-lit living room in the brick house on Church Street. He was so completely invested in his faith. And me? It was hard to admit, but I felt only halfway invested, both in my faith and my reporting.

I was supposed to be the reporter who asks the tough questions, but instead I was buying his story. I believed him—

or wanted to believe. I wanted to believe like he believed, to possess that same unconditional faith, but I wasn't quite sure my heart was wholly invested in that either, and that *was* hard to admit. The more I thought about it, the more I thought maybe that's why I was here in the first place—because I was a willing participant, willing to be won over, or rather, willing him to win me over.

J.D. told me one more story, this one about a hospital visit when his blood pressure climbed dangerously high.

"They were going to put patches on me, something in that patch to bring my blood pressure down quick, and I told them no. I said, 'I'll pray the Lord takes it down.' They said, 'He's gone completely out of his mind.'"

J.D. laughed again, and I knew what was coming, but he made me wait. The nurses had had to wait, too.

"They waited forty minutes, had to wait for the IV to drain. So when they rolled that machine in to take my blood pressure again, the room was full. Nurses, nurses aides come to see that crazy man. They rolled it in there, hooked me up, and all their eyes was glued to that machine."

J.D. clapped his hands.

"One-hundred-twelve blood pressure! They turned the machine around so I could see it. Just what I'd asked the Lord. The Lord did that for a purpose 'cause I had so many witnesses in there. He wanted to show them. I said, 'Lord, as long as you give me breath I'm gonna tell it to everyone I can tell it to.'"

I'm gonna tell it... That last quote snapped me back to the night I first met J.D., when Kernel Ken and I had come groveling for a quick story for the ten-o'clock news. *Keep telling it,* J.D. had said, thumping the armrest of his La-Z-Boy.

A year and a day had passed since then, and I felt things had changed. Or maybe I was beginning to change. Or begging to change.

I had returned to J.D.'s house on my own time when I could have spent the day doing a hundred other things. But here I was, and maybe that was a step toward greater faith. Or maybe I'd just come for a good story. I didn't know. I didn't even know if I had a story, much less the beginnings of a book. All I had were pages of notes I could barely read.

J.D. thumped the armrest again. "Every day my plan is to say, 'Thank you, Lord.' I say, 'Thank you, Lord, for keeping me through the night.' That's my prayer when I wake up every morning."

He looked at me, looked at me hard, that thin face like chiseled stone.

"The Lord will carry you through," he said, and I noticed he used the word "you." *Will carry* you *through*. I think that last quote was meant for me. Although it wasn't quite his last.

He offered his hand and gave me a firm shake. "Appreciate you coming by," he said. "Make sure you go to church on Sunday."

*

J.D. Lancaster Postscript

I called J.D.'s daughter shortly after my visit and told myself that was a start at verifying his story. But I didn't ask Carol about the miracles or to corroborate the miracles. I didn't ask her about the bird on the windowsill. I kept seeing the bird in my mind, tapping its little beak on the pane, even though J.D. hadn't described it that way. Maybe I was thinking of Edgar

Allen Poe's, *The Raven*. Or maybe subconsciously the raven was my news director, jabbing his finger at the window and demanding I get the facts straight or my reporter days were—*Nevermore*.

I know a reporter must seek the truth, and those tough miracle questions kept circling my head as I held the phone. But for now, my gut was telling me it was best to win Carol's trust rather than pry for truth. Besides, I wasn't on deadline. I could ask those tough questions later and track down the doctor and nurses and any other witnesses.

Carol was thrilled to hear I was writing about her dad. I was calling mainly to pick up a few quotes from her, but she stopped me and said, "Look, I've got tons of information I've collected. Let me mail you copies. You'll definitely want to see that."

The packet arrived a few days later, stuffed with newspaper clippings. Reporters had obviously trotted out to J.D.'s house every Veterans Day to tell and re-tell his story for the local paper.

The material was overwhelming; there was so much of it. I thumbed through the pages, reading the bold headlines. The story seemed even bigger than I'd first thought. The man was a national hero. And me? I was just a timid news reporter who'd rarely written anything more than twenty pages at a time. *Gosh*, I thought, *the weight of it*. And I didn't just mean the heavy stack. I felt his story swell—and my ambitions shrink. *I can't write a book*, I thought. *Maybe a magazine article...* The headlines screamed. *But an article for who?* I sighed and rubbed my eyes and re-stacked the pile and slid it back into the folder and dropped the folder in my file cabinet. And I walked away.

✶

I thought about that folder a lot over the next decade. I thought about it a great deal on June 25, 2010 when somebody in the newsroom said, "Hey, remember that Pearl Harbor guy you did a story on a few years ago? He just died. Think we can re-run it?"

"Died?" I said. "Oh, no."

"Whaddya mean? We *can't* re-run it?"

"Oh, yes," I said. "Please do."

As I watched it that night, J.D.'s final words sent a shiver through me: *Keep telling it, keep telling it.* There was so much *more* to tell, and I thought of the folder again—and remembered the weight of it.

I left the folder in the drawer for a few more years, and by then I *had* changed. I'd become WRAL's full-time feature reporter with two books under my belt about my colorful travels around North Carolina. I'd found my voice because I'd found my calling, but it was J.D. I credited for getting me over the hump. It was his story that put in my mind the whole idea of attempting a book.

I wondered what to write next. And then I opened that file-cabinet drawer.

I unsealed the folder and dumped the pages on my dining room table. There were articles about the *Arizona* and the landing ship but not a single one that mentioned miracles. I organized the piles, drew in a deep breath, and went to work with a yellow highlighter. And then I began to write.

I wrote using my lengthy notes from my interview with him, plus the quotes he'd given the newspaper, and when I was done I felt I'd pulled together a detailed picture of J.D. and his experiences, both harrowing and spiritual. *But my news director...*I thought. *The raven...*

"I would describe it as a dove," Carol said.

I had called her again. "Remember me?"

I hadn't talked to her in years, but time had not dulled her enthusiasm. She told me she had more information to send. "Did I tell you about his Purple Heart? Let me mail those articles to you."

"Sure," I said. "But first..." I'd put off my tough questions long enough.

"It was on the windowsill," she said, recalling that hospital visit so long ago. "The window was closed, and the bird just kept walking back and forth. I was sitting there thinking this is weird, because it reminded me of the story my daddy always used to tell about my grandfather. And Daddy said, 'Well, it's a sign. Everything's gonna be okay.' And eventually it was."

I asked whether the doctor and nurses were still around. "Oh, Lordy," she said. "I wouldn't think so."

I asked about the landing ship and the voice in the dark, and she said her dad had told her that same story many times.

"But the ship," I said. By this time, I'd researched LST-342. "Your dad said 700 men were on board and only forty-five survived." But my digging showed fewer than 300 men had been aboard and that more than half had lived. "I don't think those ships could even carry 700 men."

"Well," Carol said, and I heard her sigh. "As he got older things got confused."

I wished she hadn't said that last line, but I think I knew it was coming. I wrestled with myself to even copy the quote in my pad, and when I did I felt the crush of those words. It was as if I'd spent years piecing together a house, and just like that its integrity had been jarred loose. *Things got confused.*

Carol interrupted my thoughts to tell me how glad she was to hear from me. She said she loved her daddy and missed him and was so proud of him. She said his country, his family, and his faith were his bedrock.

She sent me a packet a few days later, another folder, but I let it sit on my desk, still sealed. I knew it wouldn't contain the answers I was looking for. How do you prove miracles? Not with newsprint.

But I'm a reporter, right? I felt obligated to look, and a week later I sat down with my highlighter, slid out the material and read about J.D. receiving a Purple Heart. The Navy had lost his records and didn't award him the medal till 2006 and then only after a compassionate nurse lobbied on his behalf. The nurse had lost her son to a roadside bomb in Iraq and felt strongly about J.D. receiving the honor he was due.

I also read about him returning to Pearl Harbor in 1966 and meeting one of the Japanese officers who'd helped lead the attack twenty-five years earlier. The officer had become a Christian—J.D. already was—and the two men embraced. "You really put us out of commission," J.D. told him.

"We woke up a sleeping giant," the officer said.

J.D. was ninety when he died, and I bet he would have saluted his coffin if he could have. It was draped with an American flag that had flown over the USS *Arizona* Memorial. Carol had included in the packet several photos of her dad, and one in particular stopped me. J.D. was an older man in the picture, and his chiseled face filled the entire page. He looked straight into the camera and smiled, as if smiling directly at me, and I wondered if there had ever been a man so full of life and faith. Once again, I thought about my own faith, how I'd grappled with it—questioned it. The freeze frame had even captured J.D.'s dancing eyes behind his oversized glasses, and it occurred to me that maybe the answers I'd been looking for were right here. I'd been looking for assurance of my own faith, as well as confirmation of J.D.'s story. How could I know they were both honest and true?

I studied the photo and thought of God and J.D. and his miracles and realized that ultimately it was all a matter of faith. In many ways, even my reporting was, too, for in the end all I had was J.D. and his story—and his smile.

But somehow it all felt right. Somehow, that was enough.

ESSAY
Touch

MIRACLES ARE ABOUT FAITH. And perhaps some are about touch.

I saw her finger slip across his thigh, just below the pocket of his khakis, a casual caress, affectionate. Her index finger, slightly bent, brushed across her husband's pant leg, a tender second or two, that's all, a fleeting moment, a whisper. I don't think he even felt it. He was busy with the bottle opener, uncapping a longneck.

We were in his kitchen—me and him and his wife and the rest of us, us guys, the four of us who'd grown up together. We'd spent every summer of our childhood in the little New England village where our parents had spent their summers and where their parents had spent theirs. It was good being back, like nothing had changed, not the place anyway, still so beautiful, so—sacred. And I don't feel that's too strong a word, not if sacred means special, comforting, precious. The place and its memories are a permanent part of me and always will be, no matter how far I might travel.

We mulled around that cramped kitchen, tilting back beers, and I was aware of the sun's slanting rays streaming through the window, shadows gathering on the countertops and walls. It was an old house, a dated kitchen with yellowing tiles his dad or granddad must have put down in the 70s or before. The kitchen stove was spotted black at the corners where its white enamel had chipped.

I stood at the island—a long-legged wooden block with ring stains from years of sweaty drinking glasses. I added another ring each time I swigged and set my bottle down.

We drank and talked and reminisced, but, really, my mind was somewhere else. I kept looking at the window, the upright rectangle with its rough wooden frame, and I grew aware of my own antsy longing. I knew that beyond the kitchen, past the family room, was his covered porch with the faded awning and wide view of Ipswich Bay. His house overlooked the ocean, our little sliver of New England coastline and one of the few places on the east coast where the sun sets over the Atlantic.

It had been a sunny day with the promise of a cloudless night, and we should have been sitting out there, soaking it in, admiring the orange ball blazing against the horizon, dipping slowly beneath the water. But we'd seen it before.

I must have seen them touching before, or at least holding hands, though I couldn't remember. But now, by chance, I glimpsed that subtle show of heart, her finger skimming across his khakis as she squeezed past to check the water or dump in the spaghetti or stir the sauce. I was standing with him at the island, my hand on my sweating bottle making another ring on the wooden block when she slipped by, and her touch was so unexpected. I feel certain there was no intention other than quiet affection, her gesture innocent—if innocent means simple, gentle. She brushed her index finger across his thigh, and then she was past and the moment gone. But the image stayed with me.

It stayed, I think, because I'd never thought of them like that, not really. They were married, of course, with three pretty daughters. But—I don't know. I think even married couples often live like they're in a cramped kitchen, jostling here and there, reaching for this and that, squeezing past one another, preoccupied, busy. I'd known him since I was a kid, a good guy, talented but humble. And I'd known her for years, too, a pretty outsider who'd become an insider, his wife of— how many years now? Fifteen? Twenty?

So why did that little caress surprise me, like it was important, that connection, as if it was somehow—sacred? Maybe that's it, her touch a physical symbol of the sanctity of their marriage. I replayed it and at the same time thought of the setting sun off his front porch, beyond reach, always beyond reach.

But she'd reached and touched. Her gentle touch—I'd glimpsed it and latched onto it, that second or two seconds, and trapped it in a container, which I locked in my head and have carried around ever since. A fleeting moment, a whisper. Like another ring on the wooden block that will always be there.

*

And there are other moments, too.

I traveled to Rome in October, 1999. I was producing documentaries then, and WRAL's main anchor convinced management to send him and a crew to the Vatican. Pope John Paul II was in his twenty-first year as pope but was seventy-nine years old and becoming frail as the year 2000 loomed.

The new millennium was a big story. People feared catastrophic computer problems or even that the world was going to end. So there was real news to report, and maybe tying it to the Catholic Church wasn't a bad idea. Thousands of Catholics lived in and around Raleigh, which made for many potential viewers. So the station gave the go ahead, and the anchor and a photographer and a local priest and I flew to Rome on a nine-day assignment.

Our priest had traveled to Rome dozens of times, knew all the best restaurants and Italian wines—he could drink a bottle by himself in one sitting—and he was friendly with higher-ups at the Vatican, which is how we were able to have the Sistine Chapel all to ourselves.

We crept in after hours, after the chapel had closed to tourists. I think the woman at the door may have even put her finger to her lips as she cracked it open and we quietly shuffled past. This was something unusual, a TV crew come to shoot the ceiling. Somehow the priest had pulled a connection, a big one—though we did have history on our side. The TV camera was High Definition, which was almost unheard of back then. We'd be the first in all of broadcasting to capture the ceiling of the Sistine Chapel in HD.

It was magnificent of course, Michelangelo's masterpiece all around us, angels and demons and billowy clouds and painted sky, lightness and darkness, his work hopeful and enlightening and frightening all at once.

It was the four of us inside that sacred dome, alone except for a few workmen standing on unsteady scaffolding along one wall. They appeared to be Italian and kept eyeing our camera.

The photographer clamped it to the tripod—the echo was as loud as a firecracker—and started shooting. The anchor and priest, meanwhile, were in awe of the art. They twirled slowly in circles, craning their necks and muttering, "Unbelievable…My God…Dear Lord."

And yet the sanctity of the moment tended to shatter every time one of the workmen clattered something against the scaffold. I'm not sure what they were working on, but it struck me as odd they weren't admiring the ceiling. I guess they'd seen it before.

As the documentary producer, it was up to me to write the words the anchor would say on camera, and what great television that would be, the anchor delivering deeply meaningful sentiments against the backdrop of Michelangelo's masterpiece. Easy for him to say.

I studied my blank notepad more than the ceiling, feeling panic instead of awe—we'd been given thirty minutes to get in and out. The occasionally clattering workmen kept interrupting my thoughts, and so did the twirling, muttering anchor and priest. "The birth of man," I heard the priest say and glanced up to see him pointing.

They'd stopped at the wall with the famous painting of Adam and God, God's right arm reaching for Adam, and Adam's left arm stretched toward God, both their index fingers extended. I heard the priest tell the anchor this was the moment God had breathed life into man, this divine moment symbolized by the two extended fingers. "But the fingers are not quite touching," the priest explained. "So close, but you see that small space? Not quite."

I don't remember the words I finally scribbled on my pad and which the anchor eventually recited. I suppose I could retrieve the old documentary and cue it up, although it doesn't much matter. The significance of those lines lasted only for the few seconds they aired and then were gone. Nobody remembers—not even me who wrote them. What stays in my mind instead is Michelangelo's painting of Adam and God and their two fingers. It's those fingers I remember. The fingers that almost—but not quite—touched.

*

It's odd how the images have become mixed in my mind, the finger of my friend's wife brushing his leg and the fingers of Adam and God. It's not just those images either, but also the Sistine Chapel ceiling and the setting sun over Ipswich Bay. Even the workmen on the scaffolding with their interrupting echoes seem linked with my friend's chipped oven, splintered window, and ring-stained wood block. They're like flaws in a masterpiece, which are also part of the painting.

We did finally mosey onto the porch that night after the sun had gone down, and it was still light enough to see boats bobbing at their buoys and the hilly outline of sand dunes at Cranes Beach across the bay. I remember thinking what I always thought when I took in that view, that it was almost *too* much to take in, so much beauty and majesty and the vastness of it all splayed before my eyes. I listened to the lapping waves and rocking boats and the wobbly dinging of a distant bell, and I wished I could absorb it all, completely, wished I could embrace it—touch it.

It's what I felt about the ceiling of the Sistine Chapel when I at last looked up from my notepad—that it was too beautiful and meaningful and overwhelming to fully process and appreciate, that even an HD camera seemed pitifully futile. *Here I am in the Sistine Chapel,* I remember thinking. *Amazing.* And then I turned to my pad again and strained my eyes at the empty page and spent more time studying it than I did the fingers of God and Adam—so close but not quite touching.

But she had touched him, and it was—sacred. In its own way, it was. She had touched him, affectionately, on the leg of his pants, and in that touch was a connection, whether *he* felt it or not. But *she* had, and the connection seemed real, and to me that simple touch signified they weren't just pawns on some kind of cluttered kitchen chessboard, but that there was a real bond between them, that the two were one—or as one as two can be.

I look inside myself and wonder if I have that same connection with my own wife or with my children. I smile when I think of them, their brown hair and brown eyes, warm eyes, happy. It's those images that play in my mind, and I'm comforted.

But what of my connection with God? Is it like the ceiling of the Sistine Chapel or the view of Ipswich Bay, so close and wondrous but just beyond reach? Have I truly connected? Or is it all at arm's length?

I have occasionally met people in my television career who've told me of miracles, that they died and came back to life or saw Jesus and were healed, and I'm wonderstruck. I'm wonderstruck because I sense they've traveled to the other side, have graced the hand of God or God's hand has graced them. They often say they aren't scared of dying; in fact, one man told me he looked forward to dying when the time came. He couldn't wait.

"Jesus," I said and stepped back.

"Jesus," he said and looked up.

Their stories stay in my mind, and I tuck them in the same container that holds the setting sun and Adam and God and their fingers that almost touch.

And hers that did.

Her simple touch in a cramped kitchen is, in my mind, linked with that profound space on a magnificent ceiling. On their surface, one is sacred, the other secular, and yet I see them as interlocking rings. Miracles seem much the same way, some awesome and large, others small and subtle. The gift, I suppose, is in recognizing them for what they are. Appreciating them—even if you've seen them before.

Her simple gesture and the nightly display across the water. The Sistine Chapel and the outstretched fingers of God and Adam. They each possess a certain sanctity; that is, if sacred means special, comforting, precious. The images are part of me and always will be—both those beyond reach and those within touch.

JOHN DERR
Of Golf and Death

"YOU'RE REALLY NINETY-FOUR?" I asked.

John Derr laughed. He had a big laugh and booming voice and talked the way a younger person might talk to an older one who's hard of hearing. But I was the younger one by almost forty-five years.

I'd been interviewing John about his long broadcasting career. He'd covered the Master's golf tournament sixty-two times, longer than anyone else in history. In 1956 he helped make history by being part of the CBS team to telecast the tournament for the first time. From '56 to '82 he served as the 15th-green announcer.

John made for another fun news feature, and though Robert by then had packed away the camera and was gathering up the gear, John kept entertaining me with stories. He wore a spiffy argyle sweater vest and pressed khaki slacks and looked ready to play the front nine at Pinehurst Number 2. Or maybe he already had.

He grabbed me by the arm and led me to a letter framed on the wall. "Arnold Palmer. He sent me that when I made the hole in one when I was ninety-two." He recited Palmer's opening line: "'What took you so long, John?'"

I was impressed, and not just by the hole in one at ninety-two, but by the personal note from a golf legend. Although, John Derr was something of a legend himself.

He'd been friends with many of golf's greats, including Bobby Jones, Ben Hogan, and Sam Snead. Of Snead, John once told a reporter: "Sam was, above all, honest. Loved money, sex, and dirty stories. Generous. Nowhere near dumb."

John was full of witty quotes and amusing anecdotes. He told me about being at his first Masters in 1935, the tournament's second year, when Gene Sarazen hit the "shot heard 'round the world," holing the ball from the 15th fairway for a double eagle that surged him into a tie for the lead and ultimately helped him win the tournament. It may still be one of the Masters' most historic moments—and John missed it completely. He'd been in the clubhouse at the time. As he put it, "When I told Gene I didn't see his shot, he said, 'That's interesting, because I've met 20,000 people who said they did.'"

I enjoyed John. He was friendly and affable. He told another interviewer one time, "I've always been pretty relaxed around the mighty. I like people, and that usually leads to people liking you back."

Indeed, John's peers had showered him with distinction over the years, honoring him with the Masters Major Achievement Award and National Golf Journalism Award. He was a founding member of the World Golf Hall of Fame, and after moving to Pinehurst in 1973 was appointed Ambassador to North Carolina and earned the Order of the Long Leaf Pine, the state's highest civilian honor.

To me, this small man with the big voice was himself like one of America's great fairways, one that rolled across decades of history. He'd met so many icons who'd bounded onto his path, and not just golfers, either: Albert Einstein, Henry Ford, Dwight D. Eisenhower, Richard Nixon, Bing Crosby, Grace Kelly, Babe Ruth, Joe DiMaggio—the list went on like some phenomenal drive from the tee. Now at ninety-four, John was able to look at his life and its wide expanse and offer some meaningful perspective. Or at least that's what I had hoped. I'd spent two hours interviewing him and his voice sounded even louder than when I'd arrived. I think he was in a hurry to get me out of there so he could hit the back nine before dark.

But something he said stopped me. He told me about his house in Maine and that he was practically neighbors with Stephen King.

"Stephen King? The horror writer?"

"Know Steve well."

Now I was gripping *his* arm. I told him how much King's book, *On Writing,* had inspired me. "I never would have written my own book if I hadn't read that book," I said. "Please tell him for me."

The King connection seemed out of the blue. And so did the out-of-body *dis*connection.

"I died and came back to life," John said.

"What?"

"Had a heart attack and died on the table, and next thing I know I'm up in the corner of the hospital room looking down on my corpse."

He might have skipped the rest and thanked me for coming by if not for my wide eyes and open mouth.

"Nurses were all around me, and they said, 'Pull the sheet over him. He's a carcass.' First time I ever been called a carcass," he said, and laughed.

My visit was rounding toward hour three and John *was* ninety-four, though with all his energy I doubted I was cutting into an afternoon nap. So I pushed him for more.

He told me about experiencing some other realm where he had good conversations with his father and father-in-law even though they'd both been dead for years. He described looking down from heaven or wherever he was and feeling sorry for everybody still living. He talked about the nurse who climbed on top of his corpse and performed CPR when hardly anybody knew what that was at the time. "She brought me back," he said. "Pretty little thing, too."

By this time, Robert had bundled his gear and was ready to go, and I think John really did need to scoot to a golf game—he still played about twice a week. But I didn't want to leave, not with the little gem of a story he'd just chip-shotted out of his memory bank—though I wondered whether it was John or Jesus who'd rolled it at my feet.

Once again, I suspected I was meant to write about these miracle stories, and that's the feeling I had when I walked out John's door. That, and another feeling—that I better follow up with him soon. Because, after all, John Derr was ninety-four.

*

He was ninety-six when I finally came knocking again, and he was not the same man. He clutched a cane and led me, shuffling, from the foyer to the living room. "Come on in, Scott," he said, his voice surprisingly still loud. Bladder cancer had not damaged his lungs—though it had attacked his golf game. "I was playing golf the week I was diagnosed," he said.

He'd learned the news in October, 2013, and now it was a year later and he didn't have the stamina to play. His voice dipped when he told me that, but not for long. "Come on and sit down, Scott," he said, as though calling me from another room and using my name to punctuate his sentence.

We sat on his couch, and I explained what I was up to, my book of miracle stories, trying my best to show this legendary broadcaster that the broadcaster next to him knew what he was doing and could be trusted. He looked at me sideways all through my meandering explanation, but John was a good sport who appreciated a good story. He'd told many of his own over the years, on air and in print. He'd written several books.

"Born October 13th. In two weeks I'll be ninety-seven!" He'd begun at the beginning and reached the end in two quick sentences. "Grew up in Dallas, North Carolina. Never went to college." He began to elaborate, and I relaxed into the cushions. "I was a high school reporter for the *Gastonia Gazette*. I was sixteen years old."

He graduated from high school in 1934 in the middle of the Great Depression, and rather than go to college he asked the *Gazette* for a full-time job. "The editor told me, 'We can pay you twelve dollars a week, but we're gonna have to charge you twelve dollars a week for teaching you.'" John laughed, even when he told me he took the offer.

He worked the police beat and wrote obituaries at the *Gazette* but especially liked covering sports, even though he wasn't able to play much as a kid because of a bad knee. "All the muscles on this left knee, they didn't come through.

I couldn't play any team sports, so while everybody would go off to play baseball, I'd play golf."

His father built him a two-par course on the family farm. "It went down from the tennis court to the apple orchard to the creek. I'd play by myself. And you know something, Scott? I never lost a game."

He left Gastonia to cover golf for newspapers in Asheville and Greensboro. The Associated Press often picked up his columns, and his writing earned him a *New York Times* journalism award.

John eventually moved to New York and in 1946 met a young woman at NBC who also knew people at CBS and helped him land a job at the other network. "Murrow hired me."

"Murrow? Edward R. Murrow?" That was almost like saying he knew George Washington, for Washington is to America what Murrow is to news.

"Oh, I played golf with Murrow many times."

He also visited the young woman at NBC many times, and though they worked for competitors, John and Peggy became partners. They married.

John worked his way up at CBS, traveling to London in 1948 to produce the Olympics, working alongside another on-air legend: Red Barber. "At the time he was the number one baseball announcer in the world," John explained. "Well, Red got sick, and CBS sent me a cable saying I had to fill in. The broadcast booth was behind the king. I had a seat behind the king of England!"

I could tell John loved sharing a good story. It made his voice rise.

"I was in Paris one time, and Murrow called and said, 'I got some sad news. Babe Ruth died today.'"

Murrow was calling to ask John to announce Babe's obituary on the radio. John had known the Babe. The baseball great had appeared on the CBS radio show many times, and John's job had been to sit and entertain him before the broadcast.

"'But Ed, I don't even know how many home runs he got,'" John told Murrow. In the end, however, it was John Derr who went on air from Paris to broadcast the death of the American icon.

In time, John became head of CBS Sports and during much of the 1950s was in charge of both CBS radio and TV. I imagined him as a friendly boss, for even now he seemed full of a kind of boyhood wonder at the world, delighted by the places he'd visited and people he'd met.

"You met Albert Einstein?" I asked. I'd read that in one of his books.

"I met Mr. Einstein in Princeton one day," he said, leaning back in the crook of the couch and staring at the ceiling, no doubt conjuring up the face of the famous scientist. I conjured him up, too—Einstein's wild gray hair and bushy mustache. John asked him if he played golf. "'No, no,'" John said, quoting Einstein. "'I tried it once. Too complicated. I quit.'"

I enjoyed sharing a good laugh with John, though it was time to start nudging him toward his miracle story. But first he insisted on telling me about someone else, and when he did his voice became noticeably softer. "The most absolutely perfect man I ever saw," he said. "The best person I ever knew."

During World War II, John was sports editor of an English-language newspaper in New Delhi, India, and became friends with a reporter named Devdas Gandhi. Devdas asked John one day if he'd like to meet his father, and John said sure but didn't give the idea much thought. In India, Gandhis were like Smiths.

Only later did he learn that Devdas' father was Mahatma Gandhi, one of the world's most revered men who at the time was leading India's independence from Britain. Gandhi's nonviolent approach would become a model for future civil rights movements worldwide.

I remembered reading about Gandhi in John's book, *My Place at the Table,* and recalled the scene when the two first met:

I was tingling with excitement. To see sitting cross-legged on the floor, drawn up to a small square table…the Mahatma himself. A nervousness I had seldom known engulfed me.

We had interrupted the old man writing, using a quill and ink on un-ruled paper…

I bent forward to shake his extended hand and he motioned for me to take a seat on the floor beside him…

I had looked forward to meeting this powerful religious and political leader, but had never considered what I could or should say conversationally.

Mr. Gandhi rescued me from my silence. He asked where in America I lived, what had been my employment, and what was my father's profession.

I was to learn that Mr. Gandhi was not an idle talker and in his presence I felt an unusual desire to listen rather than to chitchat. He had once written that, "A man of few words will rarely be thoughtless in speech… We find so many people impatient to talk. All this talking can hardly be of any benefit to the world."

John recalled for me what Gandhi had told him that day: "He said, 'John, come back to see me any time.' And that from Mahatma Gandhi was quite a thing. You felt you were in the presence of a deity. I had tea many times with him."

Gandhi died in 1948 when an assassin fired three bullets into his chest at point-blank range. John also recalled his terrible sadness at hearing the news and later meeting Gandhi's grandson: "His grandson said, 'Mr. Derr, can you tell me about my grandfather? You knew him better than I did.' And I said to myself, 'Here I am a boy from North Carolina, and the grandson is asking *me* about Mahatma Gandhi.'"

The story seemed to typify John—John-the-everyman and his long and remarkable reach, all those important people he'd met, often by lucky accident, in his many years covering sports and golf. I supposed I was just one more accidental visitor.

Or maybe my being here was no accident at all.

*

"Nineteen-sixty-nine," John began. "I was in Greensboro for the Greater Greensboro Open. I emceed the Carolina Sportswriters' dinner the night before. Had a shrimp dish and thought that might be the problem when the next morning my stomach was hurting. I went to have breakfast at the motel where we were staying and ordered my eggs and couldn't eat them, and I sweated and so forth. I decided to go back and see if I could rest, and I ran into Ray Scott. Do you remember Ray Scott? The old Green Bay Packers announcer for many years.

Well, he was one of our announcers—Ray Scott. You know how to spell Scott, don't you?"

I smiled at the quip, but John kept right on going.

"I ran into Ray and he said, 'You don't look too well. I think we better do something. Let me get hold of Cherkinian.'" John nodded at me. "You know Frank Cherkinian was our producer, you've read about him," he said as if I had. "So Ray gets Cherkinian, and Cherkinian said, 'You look sick to me. I'm gonna take you to the hospital.' And I said, 'No, no, I'm not going to the hospital.' And Frank said, 'Look, I'm calling the shots, I'm in charge, and we're going to the hospital.'

"So anyway, we get over to Moses Cone Hospital, and they take me in. Dr. Murphy Townsend was my physician, a heart doctor, and he assured me it was not the shrimp I'd eaten the night before but that I'd had a heart attack. He said, 'We're gonna hold you here for a little while, see how you make out.' And they gave me some sedatives to get me squared away and put me in a room, and I thought I was doing pretty well."

John explained it was early afternoon by then and he was due for rehearsal back at the golf tournament at three o'clock.

"Well, Dr. Townsend said, 'You might have to miss rehearsal today, but we'll see.' And at 2:12 that day I had a second heart attack, and they put out the blue alert and called for Dr. Townsend, and…"

He stopped mid-sentence.

"There's a blank spot. I can't tell you anything more that happened, not until we get into the next part of the story. But from what I understand, the doctor was called and the nurses had already been told to pull the sheet. I had no signs of life.

I had straight lined. And when Townsend arrived they said, 'You've lost a patient.'

"Well, about that time, a little nurse named Nancy who'd just come back from a training session at the Cleveland Clinic—you've heard of the Cleveland Clinic? Well, she said to Dr. Townsend, 'May I try something we learned in Cleveland called sternum massage? It's where we apply pressure on the stomach and sternum and get a heartbeat started.' And Dr. Townsend said, 'You can do anything you want to with him. He's a carcass.' First time in my life I was ever called a carcass." John laughed as loudly as the first time he'd told me the line. "Carcass!" he cackled, which made *me* laugh. We were both laughing about his dying.

"So this little nurse, freshly back from the Cleveland Clinic, got up and applied sternum massage—there was no CPR in those days—and she got a heartbeat."

"How'd she do it?" I asked. "I mean, did she climb on top of you?"

"She got up on the bed," he said, like a man grateful for his good fortune. "That's the only way you can do it. She was a good-looking girl.

"Now while they were working on me, from the time I had the heart attack until I came back to life, I was over in the corner of the room, Scott, up on the wall in the corner, and I watched the nurses working on a body, unaware it was my body they were working on. And I was feeling relief, no pain—I actually wondered why I was there—and I talked to my father and father-in-law, had conversations with both of them, and they both had been dead a long time.

"Now, they tell me when you're talking to people on the other side that it's usually a matter of seconds you're talking; there's no extended talk, so to speak. But I talked long enough to have had full conversations."

I asked him what the conversations were about, and he waved them away with his hand. "Nothing important. They were generic." But still, I wanted to know more. My mind grasped for a picture, and I pushed him for one.

"With my father we were standing on the porch of my home in Gaston County. See, I lived on a farm. My father was a rural mail carrier who died when I was in my 20s. My dad was Jay Dailey Derr. They called him Dailey. I sensed I was talking to him four or five minutes. I couldn't tell you what we talked about, but it was generic.

"With my father-in-law, I was in the yard talking under a tree. We talked about his daughter—that was my wife, Peggy."

I asked how he jumped from one man to the other, and John shook his head and said he didn't know, just that he was on the porch with his father one minute, under the tree with his in-law the next. "It was very simple," he said. "Seamless. I didn't go through a door. I didn't catch an elevator. It seemed totally natural that I talked with them in the locations I did. The conversations were the kind as if I'd been somewhere for the weekend and was expected to talk to them, and the euphoria lasted the entire time I was out. That was the thing I could never get over."

"What do you mean by euphoria?"

I half expected another quip, but this time he paused a beat and sighed, and when he spoke again he talked as softly as he had earlier.

"I'm going to tell you something now that you may have heard from some of your other people." He meant my miracle people. "I felt very sorry at that moment for the people who were living. I felt very reluctant to go back to life. I was living in a euphoric circumstance, in which there was no pain, no problem, no fear, and things were beautiful, and I said to myself, 'Isn't this great?' I actually felt sorry for people still living. It was so satisfying. I felt wonderful."

But the feeling didn't last.

"About that time, I was recovered. I was brought down from my pole up there, and they started the recovery of me from my heart attack. I went back to becoming a patient at Moses Cone," he said and laughed again. "I was no longer an angel."

Maybe he laughed to bring his story back to earth. Or so that I wouldn't think he was nuts. I suppose there's a delicate balance between the here-and-now and the mystery beyond. Except "the beyond" apparently wasn't such a mystery to him anymore. I think to him it was real, something he could *not* casually wave away.

I hoped he didn't think the conversation we were having was generic. He tried keeping the tone light, but the euphoria had clearly made an impression on him. It kept tipping the balance from humorous to serious and back again, his voice rising and falling. "I had all this experience while I was out of body," he said. "I went out of the world, Scott!"

I asked about waking up in the hospital.

"It was a couple days before I realized where I was," he said, "but waking up I had no pain." He said he decided then to keep his out-of-his body experience to himself, partly because he wasn't sure exactly what had happened; at that time, he didn't know anything about Nurse Nancy climbing on top of him.

"The explanation of it is a year later," he explained. "I came back to the Greensboro Open, had dinner with Dr. Townsend, his wife, and the nurse—Nurse Nancy—and we had a very pleasant dinner, talked about the golf tournament and that sort of stuff.

"Well, the girls—as happens with girls—got up to go to the powder room, and when they did Dr. Townsend told me the story, how he got to the hospital room so late they had already said, 'Pull the sheet over him.' They were preparing me for burial, I guess," John said and chuckled.

"Dr. Townsend told me at dinner, said, 'You made a remarkable recovery because that little girl who's been sitting over there beside you saved your life. She got up on your stomach, applied sternum massage, got a heartbeat, and once it started it kept going.'

"So about that time, the ladies returned from their visit to the powder room, and when Nancy came in I said, 'All I've got to say is, I think that's a helluva way to treat a visitor to this city. I'm there flat on my back, and you get up on my stomach and beat on my stomach, and what can I do? I'm helpless!' Told her, 'That's a helluva way to treat a visitor.' And we all laughed."

It was good to hear John laugh as he told the story. I think I heard gratitude in his laugh, which triggered curiosity in me. I wanted to know more about Nancy.

"Nancy was my entrée into the world," he said and explained how she took care of him the five weeks he was in the hospital. "Nancy was about twenty-four years old, but I fell madly in love with her. And she said, 'All heart attack patients fall in love with their nurses.'"

I didn't think John meant he was literally in love with Nancy, because at the time he was married to Peggy. I believe he admired the pretty nurse for devoting herself to his care. I'm sure he was devoted to her for saving his life.

"Nancy and I talked for many, many nights. She sat with me. She said, 'You are not going to be a cardiac cripple. Your clothes are hanging in the closet. You need to walk around.' She said, "I have saved five or six people, and at least four of them committed suicide later, and I can't understand why, what the relationship is with having a heart attack.'"

I flinched at his mention of suicide. I didn't know John back then—in 1969, I was just a kid—but he didn't strike me as being anywhere near the suicide type. As for Nancy, she seemed like a saint.

"I nurtured a friendship with her the rest of my life," John said. "She married a farm executive from eastern North Carolina and died about fifteen years ago."

I was sorry to hear that last part. Nancy had become an unexpected character in John's story, and I was busy jotting that last quote on my pad when he suddenly told me to stop. "Don't write this down." The command surprised me, and I looked up from the page. "No," he said and flapped his hand as if dismissing the whole idea of writing it down. I cocked my head at him and watched him shift positions on the couch. It looked like he couldn't get comfortable.

"She committed suicide," he said at last.

"What?"

"I know," he said. "She was told she had terminal cancer—it was incurable—but she saved many lives."

I've learned to embrace surprise as a reporter, for surprises can enhance a story and make it less predictable. A good twist might be a simple comment—some unexpected aside—or a whole unforeseen subplot. It might even be a random character who wanders into the story and changes it.

I found my voice again and asked John about the irony of it, Nancy saving lives and then...

"I know," he said. "Don't write any of that down."

My pen was poised on my pad, and it was all I could do to keep it still. I told John I wouldn't use her last name but that Nancy was important to his story and how she died was important—though I wasn't quite sure why. I needed time to think it through, fit the pieces together. Nancy's story was like a jagged edge but seemed central to the whole.

John wavered. He agreed about the irony of it, all the lives she saved while unable to save her own. He didn't want her name disparaged in any way.

"But if I just use her first name?"

He didn't answer and yet kept telling me more—while watching my pen move across the page. He talked about sending Nancy a birthday card every year, and the comment struck me. We seemed to be coming full circle. John had begun his story with two simple sentences that spoke of birth and death, and now here we were again: birth and death. "Her birthday was August 14th," he said, although death seemed so much closer, for John was ninety-six and Nancy was already gone. Her suicide seemed horribly unfair, and I felt like asking John or God or somebody why good people die, despite how cliché the question sounded. Not only that, but maybe it also assumed too much. Was Nancy's death her loss or gain? Was *she* now feeling sorry for *us*?

I had more questions for John, though I could tell his energy was starting to lag and knew our time was almost up. I asked when he finally decided to tell someone his story. "You know, about rising up in the hospital room?"

"I didn't tell anybody. I didn't tell my wife, my preacher, because I didn't think I'd be trusted. I didn't trust myself, and yet in my mind I did."

He said he waited months before at last telling his daughter. He told her one day while they were driving to their house in Maine. "I said to Cricket, 'Don't tell anybody the story because people will think I'm crazy.'"

I wondered why he'd told *me* the story, mentioning it in such an offhanded way when I'd first come to his house two years before.

"Since I've been sick I've thought of it. It eliminates all fear of dying. I do not welcome death, but I do not fear it. There's the satisfaction of an afterlife. Your body dies, but you continue on. I believe there is a heaven."

He told me about his wife Peggy dying in 1991 and about his recent bladder cancer. "They removed the tumor, but the radiation was too strong. I had to give up my car." He shook his head. "I had a heart attack about six weeks ago. Then I had one about ten days ago."

"Ten days ago?" I had no idea.

"I called Cricket who's a paramedic, and she took me to the hospital. They knew when I was coming in that it was a heart attack. My heart is ninety-six years old!"

There he was, punctuating his sentence with another punchline. He even interjected a random story about Cricket and Stephen King. "They're very close friends," he said. "We live on the same lake within a mile of each other in Maine. King was in a store, and somebody mentioned John Derr, and King said, 'Is he still alive? That SOB should have died years ago!'"

It was good to hear John laugh again, which for the moment helped ease my apprehension. I certainly would have waited on the interview had I known he'd just had a heart attack. Although I had to admit, I was enjoying myself.

"Well anyway," he continued, "King and Cricket were in my kitchen one day, and I was in the other room, and all of a sudden I hear Stephen King yelling, 'Help, help!' 'What in the world,' I thought and ran into the kitchen. Cricket was telling him an EMS story, something she'd seen as a paramedic, and *she* scared Stephen King!"

This time, I laughed just as hard as John.

He asked for his cane, which I fetched for him, and he walked me to the door—we both shuffled, stiff from sitting so long. I told him I'd start working on his story soon but that it might be a couple of years before the book came out, if it ever did. By then he would be almost ninety-nine, and maybe that's why he repeated himself just before I opened the door to go. Maybe he sensed he'd soon be departing, too.

"I felt sorry for the people who were living. Living was not easy. Dying was easy. You had no pain; you had no problems. Actually, you had no sadness. I'm very well aware of it."

His face was drawn and his eyes looked heavy, although he still possessed some energy, not to mention humor.

"I haven't checked out yet. I got a ticket, but I haven't punched it. I watch both ways when I cross the street. I live alone. I do my own laundry."

He threw me a smile and a wink.

"Cricket does the vacuuming."

*

John Derr Postscript

John died June 6, 2015, almost as if he'd planned it that way. June 6th is obviously historic, the anniversary of D-Day, and he'd told me how proud he was of his own WWII service in India. John had been awarded a Bronze Star.

He'd also died on the Saturday of the Belmont Stakes, apparently of a heart attack. Cricket went to his house after the horse race and found him in his chair in front of the TV. American Pharoh had just won the Triple Crown. As Cricket put it, "It was like he had stood up and said, 'Hooray!' and then fell over." John was 97.

He definitely did plan his obituary—the rascal wrote it himself. It traced his career and included his humor. He mentioned, for example, the priest who helped teach him how to write. John had been young and without much money but knew he needed more education. So he struck a deal with the Catholic college near his home. He would serve as the school's sports information director in exchange for a class in English. John was the only student. "I was the class dummy—but also the valedictorian."

I read John's obituary with a smile. He clearly had enjoyed living. And dying, too. He had talked of that place in the sky, or wherever he'd been, with as much wide-eyed wonder as he had playing a round with Ben Hogan or Sam Snead. I can't help but think he's up there now, meeting all kinds of interesting folks and getting a kick out of living after dying, tickled at his happy after-life.

I believe John's enthusiasm is one of his legacies. He reminded me to have fun, to take an interest in people, that everyone has a story. He even left me with some tips on reporting. In fact, he closed his obituary with one:

"A reporter can no longer be a fan, but you can be the eyes of those who are not present. They depend on you to tell them what's happening. Do it well."

John Derr did.

ESSAY
Window

1970. WE KNEEL IN THE CHURCH PEW. Mom puts her palms together and closes her eyes. Dad covers his eyes with his hand; he cups the whole top half of his head and reminds me of me when I can't figure out a math problem. He moves his lips, and I wonder what he's saying.

My legs are all scrunched up, and so I lean back and stretch and notice the bottoms of Dad's shoes, which are marked up. Luckily, we don't have to kneel too long and get to slide back in the pew.

Today there's a new minister filling in. I don't usually listen, but he starts to tell a story about a little girl who's dying, and he visits her in the hospital and holds her hand. "Will it be all right?" the girl asks. She's weak and can barely talk.

"You're going to be with God," he says.

"Will it be all right?" she asks again.

"It will, sweetheart. You're going to be with God."

"Will it be all right?"

The minister keeps repeating himself, almost in a whisper, and no one can look away. Moms are pulling out tissues and wiping their eyes. I've never heard a sermon like this before.

"You're going to be with God, sweetheart."

"Will it be all right?"

"Yes. You're going to be with God."

He says the girl finally lets go of his hand, turns her head away and stops breathing. "Be with God," he whispers.

The church is quiet except for all the sniffling, but then the minister starts again and talks in a normal voice.

But wait a minute, I think. *How does he know she's with God?* I wish he'd go back to the little girl, but he's onto something else, and soon the sniffling around me goes away and my mind wanders.

The walls at church are white, and so are the pews and altar—and even the people. But where I live in Massachusetts is also full of Portuguese people. The signs in the grocery store are written in two languages. New Bedford is the next town over and famous for whales, and a lot of fishermen are Portuguese. We have whaling pictures at home. I like the one where the tail crashes down on a boat, smashing it in half.

None of my friends speak Portuguese, but sometimes I have a hard time understanding them because of their Boston accent. We were throwing the football around in my yard one day, and somebody brought their cousin who was really good. Everybody kept shouting, "Maaatin, go, Maaatin!" After a while we chose up sides, and I picked first.

"Who you want?" the other captain asked.

"Martin," I said.

"Who?" Everybody looked at me funny.

Maybe I don't talk like them because of Mom. She grew up in Virginia and has a Southern accent. One time my friend spent the night and the next morning at breakfast poured milk and sugar on his grits. I laughed when he got ready to take his first bite. "What's wrong?" he said. "I like Cream of Wheat."

Our neighbors are Vinnie and Manny, and there's a guy named Eugene down the street who lives in a spooky green house that's leaning. Part of the roof is crumpled, and there's a huge dead tree in his front yard with long branches tangled together. I might write a short story about Eugene. I don't think he's much older than my sister, but I've never even seen him before. I hear he only comes out at night.

I also might write about the man in the pink house I see on the way to school when we drive by. He's old and bald and sits in front of his window and looks out. He doesn't smile or make any kind of face, not even when I wave. Mom says he must have had a stroke, but I wave anyway.

"Amen," the minister says, and church ends, but it takes a while to leave because everybody's talking about the story of the little girl and trying to shake the minister's hand.

The rest of the day is pretty much like every Sunday. At dinner Dad says the blessing. "Bless, Oh Lord, this food to our use and us to thy service, in Christ's name we ask, Amen." He always says the same blessing.

Before I go to sleep I think of the little girl.

∗

Today. The images come back to me, these little shades of memory that seem both unrelated and connected at the same time: The little girl, Maaatin and Eugene, the old man in the window and my friend who poured milk and sugar on his grits. *Bless, oh Lord, this food to our use…*

I shuffle the images like cards in a deck and turn them over one by one, searching for some kind of pattern. Then I flip another card, a random one that's worked its way to the top, and I hold it in front of me and consider the memory.

It's a restaurant I remember, a little building like a doublewide trailer with the word LINGUICA splashed in red letters diagonally across the front. That wasn't the restaurant's name but the specialty it served. I knew linguica was a Portuguese sausage but had never tried it. My family and I used to pass by the place without stopping.

Years later I brought my wife of Greek ancestry home for a visit—her Greek grandfather had come straight from Sparta. We drove around, and she said, "Hey, look at that place. Let's eat there." She marched through the door while I shuffled behind, wishing at the time I had olive skin like hers.

We drew some looks, but the woman in a faded apron smiled when she waited on us and didn't seem surprised when we ordered the house favorite. The linguica was juicy and spicy, peppery, and I sat there wishing I'd tried it twenty years earlier.

We drove around some more, past Eugene's house, and the dead tree wasn't there anymore and the house wasn't leaning. It had a fresh coat of paint and a new roof. "Oh, yes," my mother said later and told me about seeing Eugene at the mall recently where he'd opened a motorcycle shop. I had no idea she knew Eugene, but she did. She knew his father was never in the picture and that life hadn't been easy for him, but he was married now and had a child and the store was doing great. Mom told me he smiled when she let on how scared I'd been of him years ago.

My wife and I drove past the pink house, too, and the man in the window was gone. It was just an empty window, and I pictured him again, sitting all those years behind the glass and figured he must have died.

"You're going to be with God," the minister whispered to the little girl, and her hand slipped from his, and in that separation, he said, the human bond was broken and the eternal one sealed.

I cup my hand around my forehead and try to make sense of my thoughts, these tangled memories—in many ways, tangled identities.

I was raised in the North and influenced by the South without ever really belonging to either one. My neighbors were Vinnie and Manny, and I ate grits and picked Martin instead of Maaatin. It was as if my friends and I spoke different languages, and it occurs to me that even today I'm the kid in the pew looking at shoes, observing other people's soles. What's hard is taking a look at my own.

I'm the outside observer, the reporter who writes other people's stories—including miracle stories. "I died and came back to life," the man says.

"What?" I say and lean closer, and the divide between us is narrowed. "Tell me."

He does, and I glimpse in him a calm confidence, and the reporter in me wants to know more. The reporter seeks proof—and vindication of my own faith.

I put these miracles stories on the page but keep coming back to my own story. *God and grits?* And yet I can't quite toss the correlation aside. I think of Eugene... Sometimes kids fear what they don't see. *Eugene with a wife and child?* The revelation was like a whale's tale smashing all my preconceived notions. I never would have tried linguica had my wife not dragged me through the restaurant door.

The people who've experienced miracles tell me they've passed through a door. "I ain't afraid a dyin,'" said the plane crash survivor, and I'm fascinated. It's not the usual interview. The pattern is broken. And when patterns break, insights are allowed in.

The people on my miracle list offer me a window to the other side, but at the same time the miracles themselves separate us, as if by glass. They've experienced them, and I haven't. I remain the outside observer, the kid in the car watching the man in the window—or the Christian turning my eyes to God and fearing what I don't see. I sense in these miracle people a higher level of faith and think, *If only my own faith could be so strong.*

I must hold out my hand to God, but I question whether my reach can extend that far. Patterns are hard to break. *Bless, oh Lord...*

"You're going to be with God," I hear the minister say.

And I hear myself ask, "Will it be all right?"

MARY JUDD
The Front Porch

THERE WASN'T MUCH GREEN GRASS. I was leaving lush stretches behind with each quarter mile. Trees thinned, houses shrank, and the gray asphalt seemed to expand.

I drove by a brown apartment building with AC units jutting from the windows and a cemetery with knee-high tombstones tilted this way and that. I drove down East Hargett, past Swain and Kirkman and two dead-end streets in a row.

I passed a house with a white box stuck to the front door. Condemned, I figured. The roof was torn up, but the stringy shreds of a tattered blue tarp still clung to the back corner.

This was east Raleigh, and I drove slowly, alertly. I watched a stocky man and a boy maybe eight years old dawdle along the sidewalk next to a chain-link fence. I wondered why the boy wasn't in school on a Tuesday at noon, but at least he was with his dad—I guessed that was Dad.

This was not my first trip to see Mary Judd, and each time I felt the same way, the feeling of being out of my comfort zone, which I was. But I also noticed houses that looked different from the others. One had shiny wood trim as if bathed in coats of varnish, and I had the idea this was a neighborhood scrabbling to make good—though it could have been the other way around.

I remembered watching Mary stand on her front porch one chilly morning in February, 1997 while dozens of people huddled on the sidewalk at the bottom of her steps. Most of the men were scraggly-bearded and gap-toothed and bundled in lumberjack shirts over sweatshirts with the hoods yanked up tight over their heads. Many of the women wore their hair in bushy afros.

Mary told me most of "her peoples" were homeless, that some were drug addicts and alcoholics. I noticed one girl standing alone with her head down. She was maybe sixteen and looked bored. Or she could have been studying her stomach. She must have been eight months pregnant, if not nine.

Joining Mary on the porch was a tall blonde woman strumming a guitar, so blonde her hair was almost white. She was one of the few white people in the crowd.

Three of Mary's helpers were also on the porch, stirring a big pot of grits and arranging paper plates and plastic spoons, while the people down below breathed on their cupped hands and kept glancing up at the steam rising from the hot breakfast. I kept staring, too, especially at the scrambled eggs and sausage. It was just after 7 a.m. and I hadn't eaten. Any minute now Mary and her helpers would start serving. But first, a prayer.

"Praise the Lord! Praise God! Amen!" Mary called, then snatched a couple of tambourines and banged them together while the guitar lady strummed. "Praise God!"

Some in the crowd muttered "Amen" themselves. I admired their patience—Mary shouted and banged for a good ten minutes, and I wondered about the eggs getting cold. But at last she settled down, the guitar fell silent, and she closed her eyes and delivered a front-porch sermon, which took several minutes more. Then she waved at the crowd. "Y'all come on." Her helpers ladled the grits and spooned the eggs, and one by one the desperate and homeless climbed the steps to accept a hot meal. The food was free to them, which was why I was there. Mary had been serving people from her front porch for more than a year when somebody told me about her, and I thought she'd make a good story: A woman of meager means herself, helping those down on their luck. She relied on cash donations to buy the food so she could serve breakfast four mornings a week. God told her to do it, she said.

I noticed someone else that day—a white man in a trench coat and tie wearing a confident smile. He looked like a bank executive who'd wandered far from his office. His name was Earl, and he told me volunteers had organized around Mary's efforts. I was surprised to learn the group had a board of directors that helped raise money. I was not surprised to learn Earl was the board's president.

He praised Mary and was convinced a hot meal and encouraging prayer had made a difference. He told me about people who'd found jobs and turned their lives around—he called them Mary Judd's front-porch miracles.

I hoped I didn't frown at Earl, but I thought he might be using the word "miracles" a tad too loosely. Did finding a job really merit miracle status? I was rolling that around when he told me about Mary and an overdue bill. It was for rent or lights or heat but, anyway, she needed two hundred dollars, and if it wasn't paid immediately she feared she'd have to close the ministry.

"And that afternoon a lady drove up, didn't know anything about the bill, and gave Mary exactly two hundred dollars." Earl raised his hands, palms facing me as if to say, *I surrender*. But what I think he meant was that it was the honest-to-God truth.

A cynic would no doubt scoff at such a tale—and most reporters would pooh-pooh it, too—but I found I believed Earl. He was paid nothing for directing the board but said he was rewarded beyond measure, and he pointed to the porch.

I stood a long time watching the hooded poor accept plates piled high and couldn't shake the feeling I was indeed witnessing a kind of miracle unfold before my eyes. Perhaps that's what kept me going back to Mary. Every year or two, I aired follow-up stories. Sometimes it was a feel-good piece just before Thanksgiving. Other times it was an honest-to-goodness news item, like when city leaders ordered her to shut down. They said she was violating a zoning ordinance by feeding all those people from her house, and they won. The city forced Mary to stop.

Fortunately, a church allowed her to use a corner of its parking lot and later, one of its meeting rooms. Mary and her helpers would make the food at her house, which usually included a big pot of soup—twenty-two quarts, the size of a small tire. Mary was in her sixties then, her helpers not much younger. They'd wobble the pot to her car, plunk it in the trunk, add boxes of sandwiches and utensils, and drive it all to the church four mornings a week, praying the pot would still be upright when they got there.

The church was old and the meeting room dingy, the linoleum floor missing much of its linoleum, and the room's long table full of people who looked like they hadn't bathed in I don't know how long.

Mary made the best of it. She'd fuss about, organizing the food, eyes narrowed, concentrating hard. Come to think of it, she looked that way during the prayer, too. "Praise God! Amen." Then she'd call everyone up and begin serving.

The majority of people were men who usually bowed and mumbled, "Thank you," or "Thank you, Miss Mary," and then made their way to the table. They didn't rush but were calm, polite even. They seemed afraid of making too much noise when they pulled their chairs out to sit. Some winced at the sound of the legs scraping the floor.

Once they started eating, though, they bent close to their food as if protecting it, occasionally glancing side to side, maybe to see if anyone was watching their raw table manners. Most bent so low their chins brushed the rims of their bowls. I noticed broth and tiny bits of chicken catch in their beards, which glistened even in the dim overhead light, and I looked away.

An old piano groaned in the corner. It was about as far from a Steinway as a piano can be, its blocky wood rough and dull. A man in a floppy white T-shirt banged the keys, and Mary clapped and shouted, "Praise the Lord!" which helped drown out the sour notes. The piano wasn't tuned like a Steinway, either. "Hallelujah!"

There was no getting around the grungy desperation, though I tried to soften it by focusing my stories on Mary's compassion—but that wasn't so easy, either. She spoke in a deep voice, as if talking out of her throat, and she was sometimes hard to understand, especially when her Southern accent tangled with her country dialect.

I worked hard on my Mary stories, knowing the right choice of words could help overcome the dinginess of the pictures. Viewers generally don't like to see "dingy," and when they do there has to be some sense of uplift to offset it.

Mary had uplifted *me*. She told me she'd once been in a car wreck that paralyzed her from the waist down. Doctors said she'd never walk again. Then one day she was lying in bed when a bright light streamed in from the window and spread across her covers, and she heard a voice telling her to get up and walk. It was God's voice, she said, and she did. She climbed out of bed and walked. She said it was the same voice that later told her to step out on her porch and feed the homeless.

I didn't include the voice-of-God anecdotes in my news pieces on Mary, but they added to my awe at her supposed miracles. Plus, I liked Mary. I admired her faith and energy and never doubted her honesty. I did not believe she was feeding the homeless to help herself. Her board of directors made sure all donations went directly to the ministry.

My stories tended to bring more money in, and Mary was always appreciative. "Bless you, Brother Scott," she'd say, and I'd smile and then go about doing other stories. Months would pass, and suddenly I'd get a call. "Brother Scott," she'd say and tell me the ministry was struggling, and I'd return to

her house or the church and put together another Mary story.
"Bless you, Brother Scott, bless you."

I found I liked being called Brother Scott.

*

I rounded a corner, turned onto Cotton Place and rolled
up to 807, a small brick house with faded green-and-white-
striped awnings. There were two cars in the narrow drive, one
parked behind the other. I could have left mine on the street
but thought no and pulled in, nearly kissing the bumper in
front of me to keep my back end from dangling in the road.

I gathered my pad and pen and a little video camera I'd
borrowed from the station. I expected a long interview and
knew I could count on the camera to keep a reliable record. I
was in search of Mary's miracle stories but felt I also needed
her life story, which meant pushing the boundaries to some
extent. I'd have to get her to open up, talk about her personal
life, her family life, growing up black and poor, and her faith
in God—now that I didn't worry about, though I did fear she
might start chanting Hallelujahs and drain the camera battery
before I could really get started.

I popped the lock and climbed out of my car, and it was
probably my own hyper imagination but I had the feeling I
was being watched, that the neighbors were peering sideways
at the white man with the SUV showing up at Mary Judd's—
and it occurred to me I was already pushing the boundaries.

Dark green lattice lined the edge of the front lawn, a kind-
of flimsy fence strung with metal signs shaped like license
plates. I walked over to read them: GROW IN THE WISDOM

AND KNOWLEDGE OF GOD. GIVE YOUR HEART TO JESUS. CHRIST IS THE ANSWER.

I scribbled the sayings in my pad and then started on the skinny walkway for Mary's front door, noting all the trinkets in her yard: a cluster of cement chickens and concrete rooster and duck. I counted three birdhouses dangling from thin branches in a gangly tree and another tree with four birdhouses—and I asked myself, *Why am I counting the birdhouses?*

I also studied a tall wooden cross. It looked like somebody had nailed it together with leftover lumber and driven the end piece in the ground, then grabbed some white paint and a crusty brush and slathered words up, down, and across. I tilted my head. The perpendicular piece read PRAYER and THINGS and the horizontal one, CHANGES. I wrote *Prayer Changes Things* in my pad.

I at last climbed Mary's brick steps and peered through the storm door and saw the main door open, which probably meant she was expecting me, an inviting sign. Less inviting were the large ceramic dogs perched on either side of me, as if to guard the entrance. I wrote *pit bulls* and told myself to check with Mary later. I'm weak on dog breeds.

I reached for the knob, but a woman on the other side opened the door for me. She was black, her skin very dark, and she didn't greet me but merely turned and shouted, "Mary!" I smiled a shaky smile and walked in.

The living room was carpeted and included a couch and coffee table. "Mary!" the woman called and dashed through an archway and disappeared, leaving me alone. I occupied my time by reading the walls.

FAMILY. ALL BECAUSE TWO PEOPLE FELL IN LOVE. The letters along the arch were the peel-and-stick kind, swirly and neat, but the other message needed help. BE HAP Y WITH WHA YOU HAVE AN YOU WIL HAVE PLE T TO BE HAPPY ABOU . I figured that one might be the work of whoever painted the wooden cross.

Mary at last appeared. It had been a long time since I'd seen her, and she looked good, her dark hair combed and with a hint of auburn. She wore gold-colored earrings and a beige short-sleeve shirt. She was not petite but not heavy, either. She was solid, a woman who looked like she'd stand her ground if push came to shove.

Mary never seemed to smile easily. Her face bore a slightly serious expression, or perhaps just a thoughtful one, the look of somebody who's had to scrape and claw but who's come out okay on the other side. Or maybe that was just my own stereotypical bias at work. I didn't want to be biased, didn't want to be thought of as some khaki-wearing outsider, even though I was. I had come for a story. But it *was* good to see Mary again, and I gave her a hug.

She led me through the arch and into her cramped kitchen. A table took up a third of the room. One of Mary's helpers was busy washing dishes and another stood at the stove stirring what looked like the same tall pot I'd seen years ago. Sure enough, the faded label read 22-Quarts. I sniffed and swallowed, suddenly hungry. A red simmering soup swirled around the handle of a long metal spoon. I saw corn kernels and green beans, but when the spoon surfaced and brought up chunks of chicken I remembered the homeless men with the sticky beards and turned away.

Mary sat, and I joined her, careful to keep my hands from all the bread slices that lay on the tablecloth like squares on a checkerboard. They'd been swiped with mustard, and Mary plucked another piece from the loaf, dunked her knife into the jar and started spreading. A woman standing beside her did the same, and I noticed how careful she was at her work, coating every speck of white, even around the crust. When they finished, they flopped the slices on the table and a woman behind me slapped them with ham. I twisted my head and asked if I was in the way. She was tall, thin as a rail and white. She smiled, and I wondered if she was the new board chair of Mary's ministry since Earl had moved away. But then I cursed my own bias again and put it out of my mind.

I remembered the camera across my shoulder and propped it on a shelf by the table and pushed RECORD. I'd been told the battery wouldn't last an hour, so I jumped in.

"Tell me about the car accident?"

It was 1976, Mary said. Three of them had been shopping in Goldsboro, all three squeezed in the front seat. "On the main highway was a car coming, and we just went on out there."

She flopped another slice on the table and I winced, not at the sound of the bread but at her vague choice of words. "What do you mean you just went out there?"

"We were coming 113, just when you hit 113, and when we did we run the light."

"You ran the light?"

"We run the light, and the car struck us. I'm on the right-hand side, and the front wheel came through the door."

I pictured crumpled metal and shattered glass—and another powerful image: The red light. "So why did the driver run the light?"

"She was a diabetic and her sugar went bad, went low, and she didn't see it. We were right in front of him, so he had to hit us. He couldn't help hitting us, 'cause we run the light."

Mary kept spreading mustard as she talked, and her helpers didn't skip a beat either, though I sensed they were listening. I wondered if they'd ever heard this story.

"Had back problems, injured my head, my eyes, and I couldn't walk. It was something happened to my body, and I just couldn't use it. They hooked electricians on me, and the doctor said I wasn't getting any better, said I would never walk again. I was young, about thirty-something. He told my daddy to put me in rehab.

"Well, when they come take me to rehab they put me in the car, and when the car took off I hear the noise say something down in me, my spirit saying, 'I'm going to bless you.'"

Mary pressed her thumb to her chest.

"A voice inside me. It was something all over, a noise, like the Holy Spirit just went all in my body, and I could hear the voice saying, 'I'm going to bless you.' I never heard a voice like that before. It wasn't somebody on earth. It had to be a spirit."

I asked Mary several times to describe the voice and she kept saying it was deep down inside, till I felt we'd exhausted the topic. "So you went to rehab?"

"When I got to the rehab I was sort of sad. Lot of handicapped and blind there. I was in a wheelchair sitting a lot. Then they got me an old guitar and I tried to play a little, comfort myself."

"I mean, how long were you expected to stay? For good?"

"Well, I tell you, the doctor said for me to stay, but I had confidence. I believed I was gonna walk again, because every night after they put me to bed I would talk with Jesus. I would tell the Lord I wanted to walk again, and if he would heal my body I would serve him the rest of my days and do anything he asked.

"So after about three years, early one morning the sun was shining really bright through the window, shining over the bed I was in. I ain't never seen the sun shine like that. Shining like brass, just sparkling.

"I don't really know when I got up, but I was up, and I heard a voice went down on the inside saying, 'Look. Look back at the bed where you just got up. That's your bed.' And after that, I was just carried away. I was just happy, just carried away."

She clamped a hand on her chest and gazed at the ceiling. "Praise God. Thank you, Jesus!" I waited a moment before interrupting.

"I guess you hadn't stood since before the accident, right?"

"No, not for about three years. So right then I took a walk, but I was limping and just kind of crippled over to the phone and called my momma. I said, 'Momma?' I said, 'Come here. I'm walking.' She said, 'No, you're not.' I said, 'Yes, I am. I'm walking.'

"So in about twenty minutes my momma and daddy had drove from Goldsboro, and my momma, she was so happy to know I was walking she couldn't move. She just stood in the door and shook."

Mary suddenly pushed away from the table, rose and wedged herself in the kitchen doorway, prying her hands against both sides of the frame and wiggling as though stuck. "She stood just like this with her arms in the door."

One of the sandwich makers made a little gasp, and I did too when Mary jumped out of the doorway and began hopping across the kitchen floor like a bunny. She hopped and whooped. "Praise, Jesus! And when Momma got to where I was at, she grabbed me and hugged me." Mary shook all over and threw back her head. "Thank you, Jesus!"

I found myself sitting on the edge of my chair, hoping she hadn't hopped out of camera range.

"So after a while we got straightened out and I heard the voice say, 'Seven rounds.' Told me to go seven rounds. Momma knew what it meant, said I was gonna be healed after seven rounds. She said, 'I'll take you seven rounds,' and every round she made and brought me back I was walking better."

"So your mom was walking you around?"

"Yes. She was holding me, walking with me. She walked me to the end of the hallway, and every time she carried me down there and brought me back I was better. And that seventh time she carried me down there I walked back on my own. I run back almost, run back praising God and shouting. And Momma, she just gone out completely, praising the Lord and, oh, it was a wonderful time."

Mary shook her head side to side, murmuring to herself, and a quiet moment passed around the table. I think we all might have been feeling the spirit ourselves, or at least trying to.

The knife scraping the inside of the mustard jar is what ultimately broke the trance. One of the sandwich makers must have been overcome with another spirit, the feeling she better get busy because there were still who-knew-how-many sandwiches left to make. Mary plunked down and joined in, too, but not before throwing back her head and banging the table. "Yes, Lord!"

I liked watching Mary bang the table and shout at the ceiling, but I started feeling antsy, worried she was slinging too many "Praise the Lords!" and "Hallelujahs." Or maybe it was just me, the reporter in me pulling back the Christian in me. In a spiritual sense, I'm not sure I was all in. I admired Mary caught up in the spirit; her spirit was thrilling to watch, but I think I was riveted, not because of the glory of God in Mary's kitchen but because of the wonderful scene it would make in my book. The story was the thing. And about my story—we needed to get a move on.

I asked Mary about feeding the homeless. She said it started when she opened a prayer house in Raleigh. She said God told her to open it, and word spread. "People come from New York, everywhere, and the Holy Ghost would get all over them. People would fall out. That man was jumping that high."

She didn't explain what man but raised her hand a foot over her head. Then one day she said she heard the voice again telling her to give up the prayer house, which she didn't want to do.

"'You made me a promise,' he said. Every time I started questioning him, he said, 'You made me a promise.' So the Lord told me to go out on the street and that people would come and I would feed them. And I said, 'Go out on the street?'"

I smiled because she said it the way I would have: *Whaddya mean go out on the street?* But Mary obeyed.

"That night I cooked food. I didn't have anything but soup. Made it out of ketchup and water. I believe I had a veal bone, macaroni, rice. Whatever I had, I used.

"I went on the porch the next morning, and thirteen people came by. I said, 'How did they know?' Next morning forty-three come by. The third morning 103 came, and I jumped in the house and said, 'Lord, I can't feed all these peoples!'"

She told me she had just one pot of soup and a man helping her, and they started serving, 103 people, one by one.

"And I said, 'Is it gone, is it gone?' And the man was still feeding out that soup. And when he got through feeding all those people there was still soup in that pot."

It was the loaves and fishes story from the Bible, only this time with ketchup soup, and I wondered whether Mary had stolen the parable. Although she'd told me the story before in exactly the same way, even using the same crowd numbers.

"I guess I was a chosen child. I was always different, and my mother said I was different. My mother had seventeen children. I was the fourth child, and I was the one that break the yoke to lead the rest of them."

Mary told me she was seventy-six, but apparently age hadn't eroded her passion. "So many people in need out there," she said and told me about a homeless woman and her baby she used to feed from her porch. But then they stopped coming around and she never saw them again. "I had love for that little baby. I guess maybe she's about fifteen years old now." She said it as though certain the child was alive. "One day a guy came up. He been coming to the porch eating almost every day, but one day he looked upset, and the Lord told me to speak to him. I said, 'You come from nice family people, I'm sure you do. You got no business here. You need to get a job, go to work.' He was just in a rage, and I prayed for him. The next day he said, 'Miss Mary, I'm glad you talked to me and prayed with me 'cause I was on my way to kill somebody.'"

She told me about a time she almost had to close the ministry. "Didn't have no money, and when I get to the front door here come two trailers full of food sitting out there." It was the work of a Good Samaritan who'd come along by chance. "We were one day from closing."

I remembered the time the city did shut Mary down. The head of zoning enforcement said she was operating a business from a house, even though the "business" was a charity. He gave her sixty days to comply and threatened to fine her a hundred dollars a day if she didn't.

The zoning officer agreed to an interview, and I was ready to paint the story in black and white—until it turned gray. He said rules were rules but that he felt terrible about it and would help Mary find another place.

In time, a church came through and offered her a spot in its parking lot, and she served people beneath a tent, but it was awkward. People ducked when they entered and stayed hunched till they backed out, and then stood in the lot holding their plates and cups and trying to fork eggs at the same time.

A few months later, the city shut her down again. The parking lot was no good either, another zoning violation. So the church invited her inside. It had a little spare building, the one with the dingy dining room and has-been piano.

Mary flopped a slice of bread on the kitchen table. "They have threatened to put me in jail, but I'm not gonna stop doing what I'm doing 'cause the Lord told me to do it."

"Amen" said a sandwich maker, which set Mary going again. She raised her arms and started singing.

"Shake, shake, shake. Shake the devil off. Shake, shake, shake..." She sang the verse several times, then broke off to tell me about Kenneth who was working on a car one day and heard her outside singing that same song.

"He said, 'I like that. I like that song.' He been with me now about nine or ten years. Comes help serve food."

And so, another person Mary had reached. Another miracle. Or maybe that's not so black and white, either. *Miracle* is a powerful word, but sometimes its definition is hazy. A miracle is so often ethereal and unproven and can even be a little weird. God telling Mary to drop everything and feed the homeless from her porch? Feeding more than 100 people from a single pot of soup? I wasn't there that day, but I was taking Mary's word for it and using Earl as a corroborating witness. I told myself to call Earl and confirm the story.

I asked Mary where he lived now and recounted the sound bite he'd told me years ago on that cold morning in front of her house. "'Mary needed 200 dollars. The doorbell rang. Someone came in and handed her an envelope. Had two-hundred dollars in it.'"

"Praise God!" Mary said. "Want me to call Mister Earl? I got his phone number."

I didn't feel prepared to talk with Earl right then, more than fifteen years after our last conversation, but Mary punched the numbers and handed me the phone.

He sounded just as he had all those years ago and with that big Southern voice of his. I told him about the book I was writing. "On miracles," I said. "Remember that time you told me—?"

"Of course," he said. "It may have been the rent was due. Mary just told me, 'We're not gonna be able to make that payment,' and before I started to figure out what we were going to do somebody she didn't even know, who didn't know that story, gave Mary the exact amount of money."

I also asked Earl about the never-ending soup.

"It was a cold morning, and they were lined up all the way down the block. The pot was only half full, but we never ran out. It sort of stayed half full, and it was just like the fish and the loaves. That was a miracle in itself.

"These people," Earl continued, "when they're hungry and cold and have no place to go, they can't speak right or think right, and when well-intentioned white folks show up in that neighborhood and don't see an immediate change, we form an opinion that the people we're helping don't care. But what you realize is that every person who comes to that porch has a story, and we don't take the time to hear it. We don't have the staying power."

Earl was one who had found staying power. He'd left the business world altogether and was now in charge of community outreach for a church two hours west of Raleigh.

"I spend the great majority of my time in the inner city, and as far as serving that population, Mary Judd taught me that. Even today she'll call and say, 'This is your black sister, Mary,' and I say, 'This is your white brother, Earl.' But like brothers and sisters, we sometimes get to fussing. I used to say, 'When the end time comes I want to be standing on Mary's porch holding her hand 'cause I know she's going to heaven. And she'd say, 'I'm gonna get half way up and turn it a loose!'"

Earl was still laughing when he hung up.

I had been in Mary's kitchen a long time and leaned over to check the video camera, which showed only a blank screen, but I wasn't worried. I had a pad full of notes and felt I'd pretty well mined Mary's story. But is a reporter ever satisfied? I still needed the sandwich makers.

"She's just giving," said Gail. It was the first time I'd known her name. Before, she was just the mustard spreader in front of me, the African American woman with the round pleasant face. She told me she worked as a supervisor at a drug store—I think she'd also been counting the sandwiches. Gail said she'd been helping Mary for almost twenty-five years. "She gives her heart to whoever needs it, and many have gone out and been a good member of society. They start caring about themselves and doing for others what Mary did for them."

I interviewed the white sandwich maker, too, the one who'd been leaning over me slapping ham on bread without any trouble reaching. "Six feet," she said when I asked how tall and "Sue" when I asked her name. "Mary draws such a mix—people of faith and no faith, black, white, people of addiction. I'm struck by how many drop in. I love watching Mary. She can just say, 'Hey, straighten up,' and people are changed. I mean, me, I just couldn't maintain it, but she's a force of nature."

The "nature" reference triggered an idea. I remembered Mary's yard and all the nick knacks and knew from experience that a trivial item can hold surprising meaning. It was worth a shot, and she followed me outside.

"My brother-in-law brought them on the back of a truck," she said, pointing to the twin boxers guarding the door. So they weren't pit bulls after all. She said the dogs had to be cemented down so nobody would steal them.

"All the things I had in the country I brought them to Raleigh. Let you know I'm a country girl." We stood, admiring her concrete chickens. "Set of hens," she said. "When the tornado came it twisted that one's head off."

She pointed to a row of tiny blooms poking from the grass along the bottom of her chain-link fence. "I liked flowers when I was out in the country. Had this homeless guy dig this ditch here and plant daffodils. They come back every year, more and more."

She turned to a small tree and said it grew from seeds she'd tossed from the stoop while eating peaches. She passed her hand over its trio of birdhouses and fingered a spindly branch. "Looks like it might have some blossoms on it this year."

Maybe that's when it hit me. Or maybe it was the daffodils in the ditch, which the homeless guy had dug. Or it could have been the oversized cross with its scribbly words painted up, down, and across. PRAYER CHANGES THINGS.

What hit me was a theme that tied together the cross sections in Mary's story. My subconscious might have been at work even on the drive over when I'd seen the house with the varnished trim that stood out from the others, or the one with the tattered tarp clinging to a corner of the ripped up roof. I remembered the clinging tarp. What struck me was that despite so much despair, something tender still bloomed. What also hit me was how sappy that sounded, though it seemed true. Mary's yard symbolized it, and so did Mary herself and even some of her homeless friends.

Two of Mary's tenants had been watching us wander the yard, and she introduced me to Michael and Jodi. Jodi was white and wore a black T-shirt, and Michael was black and wore a white one. They sat on the stoop on either side of the door, and I was struck by the symmetry of the scene. They looked like they belonged there, the homeless who'd found a home.

Michael told me he was fifty-seven and had been living with Mary for months now. "Yeah, I cook all the eggs and stuff. It's been great. We just like sisters and brothers."

"We all get along very well," Jodi said. She had bushy hair and was barefoot. "I come from Connecticut. Tried to make my marriage work, but it didn't last. I used to work, but I'm disabled now. Miss Mary's been teaching me ways to be better. I help around the house—like right now, I peeled potatoes for the soup. Everybody pays rent and puts food in. Part of her rule is you gotta help clean and go to church."

I was glad Jodi trusted me with her story, but what really surprised me was something else entirely. By this time I had moved closer to the stoop and noticed her perfectly painted toenails. They were hot pink.

I thanked Michael and Jodi and gave Mary a hug, and they soon shuffled inside while I made my way to the car. Before climbing in, I took a last look around. *Seven birdhouses.* I smiled. Mary had told me the birds always come back.

A loud voice behind me shattered the peace, a bigmouth voice, hoarse and gravelly, angry and maybe crazy, the kind that belongs to somebody who's tipped the bottle too many times. I heard the voice yell, "Hitler" and "New Orleans nightmare," and turned to watch a man swagger down the street.

I riffled the pages of my notepad till I found where I'd left off. *Hitler,* I wrote. *New Orleans nightmare.* I noted what the man wore: *Blue winter cap. Sunglasses. Green jacket. Red backpack.* I don't think he saw me, or if he did, I don't think he cared. And I didn't know if *I* should care or should be writing this down. But maybe that's something Mary had taught me, or at least reinforced: the importance of paying attention. What was it Earl had said? Something about staying power. Every person has a story, and you have to take time to hear it.

"Young money, baby!" the man shouted to no one. "Watch me! Abracadabra!"

I wrote down the words and wondered what *his* story was. And whether one day he might find his way to Mary's front stoop.

ESSAY
Intertwined

JULY, 2007. IT'S A BROWN AND WHITE SPLOTCH on the lip of the roof where the shingles slope just above the gutter. It's an image of Jesus—Jesus standing, his robe flowing—or it could be.

I didn't notice the splotch until I bought a rustic little bench woven out of tree limbs. It fit nicely under the magnolia and was surprisingly comfortable, no cushion needed. The limbs hugged me and held me as I stretched my legs, pleased at the purchase. The shade was nice, peaceful. And okay, so the view wasn't the greatest—I was staring at the side of the house—but that's when I saw it: the splotch on the roof above the gutter and... *Could it be? Nah, that's not what I think it is.* But I leaned forward and looked and—*Am I crazy?* Crazy enough to jump out of the comfy tree limbs, fetch Nina, and drag her to the spot. I pointed. "Look."

Her eyes narrowed and she studied it and after a while said, "I bet that's from the old condensation line. But I see what you mean. I..." Her voice trailed off, and we stood staring in silence at the strange stain on the roof.

Is that what it is? I thought. *A stain? Or is it a sign?* And I knew what she was thinking. She was thinking about the cancer.

Nina was facing surgery and chemotherapy, and we were at the beginning of a long uncertain ordeal. We hadn't even told the kids yet. They'd been away at summer camp, and we'd just returned from picking them up.

We'd left before dawn. In years past, Nina and I had driven to the mountains, stayed at a bed and breakfast, and gathered the girls the next morning. But this time we drove straight through, and it *was* great to see them, but I noticed Nina kept her sunglasses on—to hide her tears. The girls didn't suspect anything was wrong; they were bubbling with stories about all the fun they'd had. It wasn't the right time to tell them.

We were about to head home when Nina spotted the unusual benches displayed outside a garden store. Maybe she was thinking about the cancer then, too, thinking a nice bench under a tree might be a comfort, the bench with its tangle of tree limbs intricately intertwined.

When we arrived home I hauled the bench out of the minivan and positioned it in the shade. It seemed like a good fit under the tree—across from the splotch.

Maybe I was seeing things. *I mean, c'mon, on the roof above the gutter?* I half expected Nina to laugh, but she didn't. We stared at the roof, absorbing the image—and I mean that literally; I mean trying to soak it in through our skin, crazy as that sounds.

Cleanse us, I prayed. *Free us of our fear. Rid her of the cancer.*

That night, we broke the news to the girls. "I have cancer," Nina said—such a simple statement but loaded with so many wrenching emotions. The girls cried, and we hugged, and Nina and I assured them everything would be okay. But in truth, we didn't know.

Days passed, and we met with doctors and scheduled the surgery, and I forgot about the splotch on the roof. I never had time to sit on the bench and neither did Nina. Although I did notice her looking at it through the kitchen window one night while rinsing dishes. The water rushed from the faucet onto the plate in her hands, but her hands were still while she stared out the window at the empty bench. I thought of its tangle of limbs and the first time they hugged me.

*

Today. It's been years now since that day we bought the bench, when Nina and I stared at the splotch, and if anything the splotch seems brighter. I see the outline so clearly: the head, the robe, the arms extended, the image surrounded by what appears to be a bright light. I've heard of people seeing Jesus on walls and in clouds. I think I see Jesus on my roof, above the gutter, across from the bench that embraces me.

Nina and I both have more time for the bench now. She feels good. The surgery and chemo back then were tough going, but today she's cancer free.

The girls have grown. They're busy but happy and practically adults now. I hope they didn't have to grow up too fast. Fear, I think, has a way of making you do that.

Looking back, I wish I could say my faith was never shaken. But I *did* have my doubts. I wasn't sure we could beat the cancer. And I wasn't sure about the stain on the roof.

I'd like to believe my faith is stronger now. But sometimes I catch myself staring at the splotch and thinking, *Condensation line, right. Makes sense.* But then that other side of me says, *Wait a minute, that really is the image of Jesus.* And I take comfort in that. It's like he's up there on the roof protecting us, and he's not going away. But the cancer *did* go away.

I take comfort, too, in the bench. I think perhaps I was destined to buy it that day and place it under the magnolia on the side of my house, in perfect view of the splotch. Like it was all meant to be—the bench, the splotch, fate and faith. It's as if they're all intertwined.

Yes, that's what I'm thinking now as I sit next to Nina under the tree, enfolded in the limbs, lifting my eyes to Jesus. I feel I belong here, and I know Nina does, too. She smiles. And as we offer our silent prayers, we reach out and hold hands.

And our fingers intertwine.

PHIL BRADLEY
The Survivor

THE OBIT POPPED FROM MY COMPUTER SCREEN. *August 23,* it read. *…in a hospice.* It was late 2013 and I was at my office desk, and I hadn't known—me, a newsman who hadn't heard the news. I'd Googled Phil Bradley that day only for background; I'd been thinking his story might fit my miracle book. *I had the most beautiful vision of Jesus Christ,* the obit read, and I figured the writer must have dug up quotes from old articles; Phil Bradley had given many interviews over the years. *And I have never had a moment of fear since.* His harrowing ordeal made for a compelling story. *And I've had thousands of people ask me how come I survived.* I had asked him that question myself more than once and now sat wishing I could pose it again. But I couldn't, because Phil Bradley was dead at… *age 87.* I shook my head. It was hard to believe. He was a survivor; that's how I'd always thought of him. Even his death notice pointed it out. The obituary's headline ran two lines long:

"He was the only survivor of the crash of Piedmont Airlines Flight 349 on Bucks Elbow Mountain above Crozet on Halloween eve in 1959."

✳

That morning, Halloween-eve, Flight 349 idled on the tarmac with just one empty seat left on the plane, way in back on the right-hand side.

"Suppose you were already in that single seat," Brad said and pointed at me. He often went by Brad instead of Phil, Brad for Bradley. It was 1995, and we were seated across from each other, and I hadn't expected him to do that, point his finger as if I'd been in line to board the plane, too, even though Flight 349 had taken off three years before I was born. "Suppose you were and I was in another seat? Would you have lived and I died?"

The question hung, and he seemed to mull it more than I did—I think he'd been mulling it half his life. "I think about that every day," he said at last.

Brad was stocky: big head, broad shoulders, a perfect middle linebacker had he been fifty years younger. I interviewed him again in 2002 and a third time in 2011 when a photographer and I were about to leave for an overnight trip to Charlotte. I remembered he lived in nearby Monroe and couldn't resist. He told such a great story, but when I reached for the phone I hesitated. *What kind of crazy reporter would keep reporting the same story three times over?* I called him anyway.

We'd kept in touch through the years, though it was usually him calling me. "This is Brad," he'd say. "Just checking in." His voice was husky but friendly. One time he told me about a book he was writing about the plane crash. Several times he called to tell me about a memorial he was planning. "So the people who died won't be forgotten." He was designing it himself. "A granite stone, three-feet square, four-feet high with the names of all those twenty-six people."

I think he was surprised when I called him that day in 2011. It had been a while since we'd talked, maybe even a couple of years. "Hate to ask," I said, "but can I interview you again?"

"Sure," he said in his playful growl. "Third time's the charm."

*

On October 30, 1959 Dwight D. Eisenhower was president, John F. Kennedy was a senator, and E. Philip Bradley a businessman. He was thirty-three years old, a labor organizer who'd spent the last several days at an AFL-CIO meeting in Oklahoma City. But now it was Friday, and he was returning home to Virginia. He awoke at 5:00 a.m. prepared for a long day of travel, one that required multiple plane changes and stopovers. Flying back then was often a daylong event.

Brad's first flight took off at 7:00 a.m., stopped in Tulsa and flew to Chicago where he was supposed to change planes, but there was bad weather in Chicago, which caused a long delay. He sat and waited and finally boarded, but by the time he landed in Washington, D.C., it was already nightfall and his connecting flight had left without him. He was in luck, though. Roanoke was his final destination, and there was another plane due to leave Washington National at 7:30—Piedmont Airlines Flight 349.

It was a DC-3 that had logged more than 26,000 flying hours over fifteen years without a single serious incident. Piedmont had nicknamed it the Buckeye Pacemaker, and its routine route was Washington to Roanoke with stops in Charlottesville and Lynchburg. Piedmont had formed a decade earlier in North Carolina, and its debut fleet was all DC-3s. Each plane carried about two-dozen people and offered several first-time features. Passengers could, for example, pop on their own overhead reading light and adjust the air circulating around them. The cabins were roomy and quiet, but best of all was Piedmont's safety record. None of its planes had ever crashed.

"Because of weather, I was late coming out of Chicago and put on standby," said Brad. "The only seat available was a single seat in the right rear."

He first told me his story in 1995 while sitting in an Italian-style villa on a Virginia mountaintop. I was living in Richmond then, in charge of a magazine show for Public TV. I had read an article about him and tracked down his number.

His easy manner on the phone made me feel like I already knew him, which was a relief. Call the sole survivor of a plane crash and you don't know how he'll act after living through such an ordeal. But I didn't detect any jitters in that deep and jovial voice, only a hint of hesitation. He'd become a federal mediator by then with a busy schedule—although it occurred to him he'd be crossing through Virginia on an upcoming trip, and he suggested meeting someplace convenient for the both of us.

We settled on Swannanoa, a fifty-two room marble palace with tiffany windows, gold plumbing fixtures, and a domed ceiling. It sat high on a hill in Afton, Virginia, the first home in Nelson County to have electricity.

Even the name "Swannanoa" sounded lofty and ethereal, spiritual, and maybe a little cultish. At that time, the house belonged to the University of Science and Philosophy, a group dedicated to the "upliftment of mankind." I wasn't sure what I was getting into when I called to ask if I could borrow a room, but the woman on the phone was pleasant when I explained the story. I suppose it qualified as "upliftment."

Afton Mountain is known for dense fog. I'd driven across it before, often slamming on brakes while fender benders blinked out my window like crippled ghosts. It was either an appropriate place to meet Phil Bradley or the worst place possible: Foul weather, a rugged mountain, and mangled metal. If he suffered even a trace of post trauma, I worried Afton might trigger a full-blown flashback.

But fortunately the weather was clear the day we met and Mr. Bradley very likeable. "Brad," he told me, though I was tempted to stick with Mister because he was my parent's age and wore a blazer and tie. And yet he was down to earth, even in a palace.

Our shoes echoed against the hard floor when the woman who greeted us led us across the palatial foyer. I was sure it was the same woman I had talked with on the phone. Her gentle voice matched her petite frame, and she moved with a graceful step; most of the echoes, I think, came from Brad and me—and from John, the photographer who'd joined me on the trip.

But the clodhopping stopped when we entered a side parlor with thick carpeting. It was a nice room with handsome pieces of furniture, and the light was soft and cast a yellowy glow. The woman bowed and gestured with her hand as if to say *It's all yours,* and when she closed the door behind her, she did it so softly it barely made a click.

"It was October 30, 1959," Brad began once we'd settled in our chairs. "Taxied on out and took off runway thirty-three, I remember."

He was completely at ease and seemed glad somebody was interested in his story. I think he was enjoying the Italian villa, too. "Everything seemed to be normal. Engines were generating good power."

His calm actually heightened the tension. It was the classic "everything-normal" storyline that's a sneaky build up to the inevitable haywire that happens later. You just know disaster looms, and how odd that the calm before the catastrophe ratchets the anticipation. He may have worked as a labor mediator, but I think Brad also enjoyed telling a good story.

He did in fact write a book a few years later, a self-published hardcover with a picture of a Piedmont DC-3 and a long title written in red: *The Crash of Piedmont Flight 349 into Bucks Elbow Mt. as Told by the Sole Survivor, E. Philip Bradley.*

I read Brad's book and interviewed him twice more; those other times were when I was at the network affiliate in Raleigh—same story, same station, but separated by several years. Thankfully, viewers tend to have short memories. I did those interviews at his house in Monroe, which was certainly different from the palatial Swannanoa. It was dimly lit inside with well-worn furniture and nick knacks crowding the tables and mantelpiece. The room felt comfortable; I think *he* felt comfortable. Each time, he took me once again through the story, occasionally adding new details.

I was able to piece together Brad's account of surviving that flight with the details he both recorded for me on camera and wrote down on his own. He was a survivor; I still think of him that way, for even though he's gone now, his story survives— at least on the page. And so does his miracle.

*

"The last thing I saw in Washington was the Washington Monument. I remarked to a lady on the aisle seat across from me that the lighted monument was a beautiful sight. She responded, 'Yes, it is.' Those were the only words I exchanged with any of the passengers."

I imagined the scene and figured it must have been peaceful for Brad, watching the lights twinkling out of the darkness below, enjoying the natural quiet of the night, soothed by the hum of the engines.

"Not too long after leaving the ground I could see the anti-collision light on the tail of the aircraft bouncing off the clouds, and I was just sitting there looking out the window. But before that, I had purchased a book—*Exodus*—in Chicago."

I looked up the book later. "The tale that swept the world with its fury," blared one review. At the time, it was a bestseller.

"I had only read thirteen pages coming down from Chicago. If you're superstitious I guess you would have read one more page anyway." He threw me a wry smile before continuing. "Lights had gone on. You know, fasten seat belts, no smoking. Just a normal flight."

The flight from D.C. to Charlottesville was supposed to take an hour, and when he sensed they were getting close he leaned over and looked out the window again. He knew the area from having grown up nearby and recognized several landmarks below: a big intersection in Culpepper, Virginia, and then the Barracks Road Shopping Center in Charlottesville. The shopping center was new—Charlottesville's first suburban strip mall. In fact, that night it was celebrating its grand opening. A band was playing and a searchlight swept the sky—many wondered later whether the bright beam confused the pilot.

Brad told me later he didn't think so, although he did find it odd when the plane began looping the area. "One or more complete 360-degree circles over Barracks Road," he said. His watch read 8:30 p.m., which was their landing time in Charlottesville. But to Brad's surprise, the flight attendant began pouring coffee for the passengers. He figured that meant they weren't going to land in Charlottesville but instead go on to Lynchburg.

Except a short time later, the pilot lowered the landing wheels—the whine and thud reverberated through the cabin. "Then I thought, again, why the coffee if we're landing in Charlottesville?"

He looked around at the other passengers, but no one seem concerned; in fact, just the opposite. "Somebody had apparently just told the punch line to a joke in the middle of the plane on the left-hand side, and those people were all laughing."

Then came another sound—a loud scraping. "I heard the wings hitting what I assumed were trees, and I immediately started to duck down and looked at my watch. Twenty minutes to nine. 8:40."

He said the plane shook violently and described "a terrible lurching noise," which was probably the trees shearing off the right wing. "A tearing crunching sound of metal."

And laughter.

"That was the last sound I heard from any of those people. They were all laughing when that plane hit the mountain."

Brad kept his eyes on me, and there was no spike in his voice despite the growing drama of his story. "And the next thing I know, a tremendous amount of noise and impact."

The force ripped every seat loose from their bolts in the floor. "Including my seat," he said. "I stayed in my seat, fastened by my seat belt, and was propelled through the aircraft and thrown from the plane when the fuselage section broke open. I was going through the air so fast and remember hearing a loud roaring sound like an ocean of angry waves breaking on a beach, and the next thing I know my face smacked the ground, and I'm getting dirt and leaves in my mouth."

A ludicrous vision popped in my head, of Brad in suit and tie screeching through the air like a seated Superman, then plunking to earth and skidding across the ground. But soon, that vision vanished and another figure took Superman's place.

"After I'm getting dirt and leaves in my mouth I see the vision of Christ standing there, I'd say thirty to forty feet away from me, what I think we all think Christ looks like, with his arms spread out real wide you know, and it illuminated the side of that hill."

Brad didn't hesitate in telling me what he saw, didn't seem worried about what I might think or embarrassed—if that's even the right word. He never looked away and spoke in his same even manner.

"The Christ figure had long brownish-black hair and beard. He was dressed in a long white robe, and he stood suspended three to four feet above the ground. He stood barefoot, his arms outstretched and his hands turned upward. I can still see his piercing eyes focused on my eyes and the movements of his mouth as he spoke: 'Be concerned not, I will be with you always.'"

Brad repeated the phrase.

"'Be concerned not, I will be with you always.' I could see his eyes blinking and his lips moving."

Jesus blinking? I'd never considered Jesus blinking.

"Immediately the Christ vision disappeared from my sight but has remained embedded in my memory."

I leaned forward in my chair, clasping my notepad, and asked him to take me through it again, exactly what he saw and heard.

"I could see his eyes looking right at me, and then his mouth." Brad traced a finger along his lips. "I could see his mouth when he said to me, 'Be concerned not, I will be with you always.'"

I never did open my pad; I never felt the need. I knew I'd remember the words without having to write them down.

There wasn't much left to ask, and I think Brad felt the awkward silence, too. He looked past me out the window and spoke the words again, more to himself, I think, than to me. "Be concerned not, I will be with you always." Then he looked back at me and smiled.

"Now that's a heck of a message."

✳

E. Philip Bradley grew up in the Allegheny Mountains of Virginia, in the busy railroad town of Clifton Forge. One of his first jobs was cleaning out stables at Blains' Dairy. The Blains paid him, not with cash but with manure, which Brad would shovel into a wheelbarrow and roll to a neighbor's house. He'd earn fifty-cents for a load.

In the summertime, he managed a boat dock and store at a state park nine miles away. On Saturday nights he'd walk home so he could be at church the next morning to serve as altar boy, and after church he'd walk the nine miles back to the park.

When Brad was sixteen he caught pneumonia and missed so much school he never returned. Instead, he took a job with the railroad, and a short time later, in 1943, enlisted in the Navy. "I felt I had a duty to go," he said.

He had served about a year when his ship took orders to cross the English Channel. Brad didn't realize it then, but D-Day was at hand.

"When we arrived the next morning and dropped anchor, that became the Omaha Beach invasion."

His job was to help shuttle men to the beach—many of whom died soon after stepping off the boat. "So many Americans gave their all to protect our freedoms," he wrote later and described that time as "the worst reality-of-war experience one could encounter."

As it turned out, D-Day would help prepare him for his worst reality-of-*life* experience yet to come.

✳

"Be concerned not, I will be with you always."

As I sat listening to Brad, another phrase kept whispering through my head: *Be careful.* An itchy group of news managers elbowed their way into my mind, frowning and picking at my sole survivor script. Granted, they loved stories with powerful moments. But a vision of a floating Jesus? Uttering stilted dialect? They'd demand corroborating witnesses. And yet, what else could I offer? In this case, there was only Brad— and maybe Jesus—on the side of that mountain. Everyone else was dead.

"It happened so suddenly," he continued. "We were probably going 160-miles-an-hour when we hit that mountain."

The enormous force flung Brad through a tear in the metal as the wrecked plane hurtled 150 feet through the woods, its fuselage breaking in two. He hit the ground hard, finally landing near a boulder. The brush was thick, the area remote, and yet the town of Crozet, Virginia, was just two-and-a-half miles away.

"Takes a little while to figure out what happened. Then you start into the mode of, *Is there anyone else alive?* I called out to see if anyone would answer me, and nobody answered, nobody screamed, no hollering, no crying out or anything. But shortly after the accident I could feel this fella's leg off to my left, and he never made a sound, and I thought, *Well, maybe he's unconscious or something.* But he'd been decapitated, as had thirteen of the twenty-six people killed."

I winced at the grisly detail.

"But you know at Normandy I saw a lot of death, and not to say that kind of stuff helps but maybe you understand it a little better. Of course, I have a lot of determination, and it takes a lot of determination and a lot of never-give-up. The thing of it is, I just felt optimistic, and I felt no fear and that at some point somebody would come. I was just that sure."

He snapped his fingers, and I marveled again at how unexpected the telling of his story was. He was not emotional in the way crash victims might be, and yet his straightforward tone was no less compelling.

"I checked myself for internal injuries and lacerations and didn't feel any, and I thought, *Well, I'll be dog, I'm gonna be able to get up and walk away from here.* So I took the seat belt a loose and started to get up, and that's when the first pain hit. And it was tremendous pain; in fact, that night I prayed to go unconscious. It was terrible. My hip came right out of the socket and turned so that my left foot was just the opposite of my right foot." He demonstrated with his hands, pointing one up, one down. "I couldn't do anything. I just had to lay there and hope somebody would come find me."

He noticed little fires flare up, probably electrical or battery fires, but they soon went out. All was quiet, and then a cold rain started falling.

"I was getting right thirsty and held my mouth up to see if I could get any water, hoping it would hit me in the mouth. Hit me everywhere but in my mouth." He cracked a smile. "I was on a diet anyway, so it worked well for that."

He told me about twisted pieces of airplane dangling in the trees above him. "The wind was blowing around, and every once in a while I could hear parts of metal falling." He'd lived through the crash but now worried about getting bonked in the head and dying if the wind blew too hard. "I got to thinking there could be an engine up there, fall on me, hit me on the head, kill me." He cracked a smile then, too.

"That first night it was right chilly." He glanced around for something to use as cover and noticed a coat caught on a tree branch above him; it looked like a crew member's coat, and he grabbed a stick and managed to yank it down. He also clawed for a nearby seat cushion. "And I put my face into the back of the seat to keep my face warm."

He learned later the temperature that night dropped to thirty-eight degrees. At one point he heard sounds coming from the underbrush, and then a "high-pitched, blood-chilling howl." He realized there were wild cats in the woods and worried they might be hungry and come after him, but they never came close.

He heard cars whizzing along a distant highway and the rumble of a faraway train. "Those were comforting sounds and helped me hold on." He was cold and exhausted, hungry and thirsty. "I thought of my family, how they must be worried about me and why it was taking so long for the rescue team to come, if in fact they would ever come."

The night passed slowly. "I constantly battled with myself to stay in control and not allow doubt to take over."

Saturday morning dawned at last, raw and dreary. It was Halloween, and the grim daylight revealed the enormous carnage.

"I didn't have any need to look at them. I saw enough of that at Normandy; that was a mess on Omaha Beach that morning. Good Lord, have mercy."

Before the fog lifted, two bears moseyed up. "A big one and little one, and the big one stood on its hind legs and looked to me six, seven feet tall—the little one, hopping all around—and I thought, *Keep going, you fuzzy rascal. Don't come over here. I got enough problems.*" The bears eventually wandered off.

The fog lifted and soon Brad saw planes fly over, but the foliage camouflaged the wreckage. Plus, the plane's emergency transmitter had failed, so it never sent a signal that could have helped teams locate the site. All Brad could do was lie there, helpless. His twisted feet hurt worse than ever, and as the hours dragged by he began to think he might die a more painful death than anyone else had in the crash.

"Later Saturday night I tried to occupy my mind by reminiscing about my navy experiences." He also thought about his upbringing. "How my parents had taught family values, moral values, that wherever life took us we should never be willing to surrender for any price."

Saturday gave way to Sunday, the first of November, and Brad woke to find a lone turkey vulture peering at him from a tree limb.

"He was the lead man, I reckon. He came in early and looked around and left. About an hour later there were literally dozens of buzzards, and they just sat on the tree branches and stared. I found a stick and kept moving it, making sure they saw it."

A veterinarian told Brad later that if the buzzards had realized he couldn't fight back, they probably would have swooped down, pulled his eyes out, and feasted on him. "Fortunately, that didn't happen," Brad said and grinned.

What I saw so often in Brad's eyes was a playful gleam, but playful not in the sense of trivializing what he'd endured. It was similar to what I saw when he told me about seeing Jesus. Brad radiated contentment, though there was something deeper, too. I think the look I saw was one of gratitude.

The search team numbered 1000, but it wasn't until early Sunday when a crewman aboard a Marine Corps helicopter saw what he thought was a gash in the woods below. He asked the pilot to circle back, and that's when they spotted the plane's tail section. It wasn't long before Brad heard the forest begin to rustle.

"Sunday morning I started hearing somebody hollering to somebody else, 'Do you see anything yet?' And the guy hollered back, 'No. Do you?' And I thought, *Well, that's above me.* Then I realized they were rescue people. I said, 'Hey, over here's the plane wreck.'"

One of the men hurried over. "And I said, 'Where you guys been?' He said, 'Oh, we been lookin.'" Brad told the man he was okay and asked him to see if anyone else was alive. The man came back five minutes later and said he couldn't be sure yet, which only helped confirm what Brad had long suspected. He was the only survivor.

"And within, seem like to me, another five or ten minutes, the whole side of that mountain was just full of people."

Brad handed me a collection of black-and-white photos, which showed dozens of men in jump suits and caps, along with bodies covered in blankets on the rocky ground and crumpled pieces of plane wedged within the trees—the rescue had been well documented. The pictures also showed a young man on a stretcher.

"I asked how they planned to get me out, and they said, 'Well, the only way will be to carry you to the top of the mountain.' I said, 'That's fine, except you're gonna have to give me some morphine or something before you move me.' So they gave me a shot, waited a little while, and then gave me another one. I think twenty minutes after that I could have got out of there by myself. I felt good. I was ready to go."

He laughed, and I did too at the fun he was having in telling the story—or maybe it was the relief he still felt all these years later.

"They eventually put me in a wire basket and strapped me down. I'll never forget, there was a cameraman standing off to my right when they were carrying me up the mountain, and I thought I knew him. I said, 'Hey, how you doin'?' like that." Brad gave the man a little wave—and to demonstrate, waggled his hand for me as well. "I realized I didn't know the fella, but he said, 'Would you do that again?'" So Brad good naturedly tossed him a second wave. "I was in a pretty good mood going out of there. And the cameraman took a picture. In fact, he got a national award for it."

It *is* a good picture. Brad showed it to me, and I've studied it since. There's the lazy wave and a young Brad with a blanket pulled to his chin. His head lolls to the side and his eyes appear half open. But the eyes, I think, are deceiving. It's not the dazed look of a weary man, for he gazes directly at the camera; it's almost a hardened stare. The wave might say, "Hey, how you doin'?" but the eyes demand, *Look at me, I made it.* I don't think the look was staged at all.

The climb to the top was steep and rugged. Volunteers talked about it later, how the National Guard and State Police had to string ropes to hold on while removing the dead. Some of the bodies tumbled off the gurneys on the way up.

"The way they carried me from that crash site to the top where the helicopter landed, that to me is durn near a miracle. When they got ready to put me in, the pilot was standing there, and I was kidding with him. I told him since I had made it up from the site I didn't want him to crash and make it two in a row for me. He said not to worry, I'd be all right."

The helicopter took off for the University of Virginia hospital and set down on the football field at Scott Stadium. "Around the fifty yard line," Brad said, and I made note of the detail.

"They put me in a rescue-squad truck and started off, just flying. I think Richard Petty was driving. I told him, 'Slow down; no hurry. I been up there almost two days. No rush to get to the hospital.'"

He leaned forward and looked me in the eyes and then down at my pad. I think he wanted me to be sure I got this next part right. "I'm told that was the first commercial airline crash in the country where there was one survivor."

I told myself that was a statistic I'd have to research, and I did later but had trouble nailing it down—although if Brad wasn't the first lone survivor, he was certainly one of the first, no doubt.

But other research proved hazy, too—like what caused the crash.

The Civil Aeronautics Board learned of the pilot's strained marriage and psychotherapy treatments and ruled he "was so heavily burdened with mental and emotional problems that he should have been relieved of the strain of flight duty." But the official cause of the crash, it said, was that the plane failed to change course. It should have made a twenty-one-degree turn but for some reason didn't. The board noted the pilot's habit of keeping the lights on his instrument panel low and suggested that maybe he and the co-pilot didn't see how off-course they really were. Instead of approaching the Charlottesville airport, they headed straight for the mountain.

Another reason they were so off course could have been radio interference. The Airline Pilots Association looked into the crash later and disputed many of the earlier findings. It found that pilots had often complained of erratic signals around Charlottesville, and when investigators checked they were dismayed to pick up an overriding signal from a private airport in Hagerstown, Maryland. They went further and conducted two flight tests to see what would happen without a ground signal from the airport at all. According to the Association's report, had the test planes kept flying, "both flights could have expected to crash on Bucks Elbow Mountain within a few feet of where Flight 349 crashed."

The Association also questioned whether the pilot of Flight 349 was in fact suffering emotional distress. It learned the psychotherapy treatments were actually marriage-counseling sessions. The pilot's son said his parents had agreed to reconcile just days before the crash but that the government paid no attention. "They always blame the pilot," he said.

Blame wasn't part of Brad's story; at least, I didn't think so. He seemed to accept whatever happened and dealt with it as best he could.

At the hospital, doctors said Brad's dislocated hip was one of the worst they'd ever seen. They struggled to twist it back into place and finally laid him on the floor and used their weight to apply more pressure. "That worked," Brad said. "I could feel my hip going back into the socket."

Doctors also worried about his mental condition, but he showed no immediate signs of anything wrong. "I even watched the Redskins play the Pittsburgh Steelers that afternoon," he told me, and my ears perked up. The Redskins are my favorite team—I was tempted to ask who won.

He spent six weeks in the hospital, and one day the nurse who regularly bathed him and changed his bed probably did question his mental stability.

"So this particular morning she left, and all of a sudden I feel something biting me. So I looked down. There were hundreds of red ants all over me, just eating me alive, and I pushed the button. She wanted to know what it was. Said, 'Mr. Bradley, what is it?' I said, 'Before I tell you what it is I want you to know I am not crazy, but I've got ants here eating me alive in this bed.'"

It turned out, construction was taking place in the hospital, and the vibration had apparently unsettled the ants.

"I guess they decided to make a new home in my linen closet. So the nurse sent an orderly in with one of these fly-spray cans, and he sprayed me royally. Needless to say, I smelled like kerosene, and the only thing I thought about was, 'My Lord, I gotta take another bath now.'"

The anecdotes kept coming, especially now that our talk had moved beyond the crash, though back then he still faced some tough times. He developed blood clots in his legs and contracted pneumonia. "I overheard the doctors discussing my situation, and it was stated that they were going to do all they could for me but did not have much hope."

But Brad gradually improved, and on Christmas Eve morning the hospital finally discharged him. Times were different back then—he had to arrange his own transportation and hired an ambulance from the funeral home back in Clifton Forge. When Brad met it at the curb, the engine was off, the back door stood wide open, and the inside was frigid. "I had just gotten over pneumonia a few days before."

To make matters worse, snow began falling and picked up during the 100-mile drive. At one point the driver got lost, and then the ambulance ran out of gas, conking out on a blind curve just four miles from Brad's house. He feared a car might round the corner and plow into them, but fortunately the rescue squad arrived and drove Brad the rest of the way.

He'd left the hospital at 8 a.m. and didn't arrive home until 5:30 that night. His friends had gathered earlier for a big welcome party, but when Brad didn't show they gave up and left. "Which I have always regretted," he said. "By then I was so emotionally drained and exhausted I broke down and cried uncontrollably."

He told me of his long painful recovery and the question he kept asking himself: *Why did I alone survive the plane crash on that fateful night when so many people lost their lives?* He said he didn't know the answer and had long ago given up searching for it.

"No, I don't view life any differently now than I did before that I'm aware of. You go through something like that and you can go through life wondering about things, and maybe it's the Lord's will I was the one to come out and maybe not; I don't know. Who knows? Nobody knows. It just happens. And so you just accept life as it's meted out to you. Life to me is pretty. I just enjoy life. I think life was given to me up on the side of that mountain."

One day Brad called me and said he'd decided to erect a monument at the crash site so the people who died would be remembered. He said he was going to design it himself and raise the money. He told me he'd visited the site, a tough hike over rugged terrain, and was amazed to find the wreckage still there, although much of it had been vandalized over the years. "But the fact the DC-3 still lies on the side of the mountain is remarkable," he said.

He took pictures and included them in his book, photos of him peering through the jagged hole of an engine part and leaning on one of the plane's landing wheels, which came nearly to his waist. Memories came back to him, too.

"Remembering my painful and lonely hours and all those silent and broken bodies scattered around me. I will always question the tragic ending for so many people in such a desolate place, many of whom were only a short distance from their homes and families."

But he never questioned the vision he said he witnessed after the crash. "I think we can all agree those people saw him, too. He was there for them. He took them with him. I believe that."

Brad called me again later to say he'd finally done it—the monument was in place at the base of Bucks Elbow Mountain, near Crozet, about a mile and a half from the crash site. He invited me to the dedication ceremony, which would have made for a great follow-up, but I wasn't able to make it. For reporters, there's always another story, and time slips away; you don't have time to dwell on the ones you've already done.

Once they air, you tuck them in the archives and move on. But sometimes the pang you feel for an old story lingers.

"People ask if I've felt guilty being the only survivor. No, I don't feel guilty. The good Lord made that decision; I didn't make it. And so I live with that every day, and it's a great feeling to have. I haven't had a worry or a fear since."

In fact, some twenty years after the crash he earned his pilot's license, logging almost 2000 hours in the sky. As Brad put it, "I figured if I went down again it would be my fault."

He also erected that monument, and I could tell he was proud of it when I interviewed him that final time in 2011. Brad was 85 years old then and told me the more he aged the more he thought about the victims. He felt the monument was an appropriate way to honor them. And not just them.

He said he'd made the granite marker three-feet square and four-feet high because Jesus was three to four feet off the ground when he'd seen the image illuminating the mountain. He designed the monument's top so that it tapered to a point. "A twenty-degree peak," he said, "like his arms were going to heaven. That's how I arrived at the size of the stone."

He told me he saw Jesus one other time years after the crash. It was the middle of the night, and he awoke suddenly and sat up, and there was that same vision at the foot of his bed, but this time it was silent. "He was there, and just like that he was gone," Brad said and snapped his fingers and shrugged.

*

I thought about Brad's vision of Jesus after reading his obituary. I thought about the here and now and the here and gone. It was hard to believe Brad was dead. I'd heard his story three times and sat wishing I had yet another chance to interview him. Though I'm not sure he would have added anything new. Brad was a roll-with-the-punches kind of guy, and I think he'd delivered all the details he could about the crash, and now he was on to his next adventure. I smiled when I thought of that, Brad ambling around heaven, mingling with the folks up there, adding a little humor to the world above. I bet he also felt good about leaving something of some permanence behind. He'd erected the monument and written the book—though I wondered how many people visited the monument or read his account, and I began to think maybe I should pick up where Brad left off and leave something behind as well to help preserve his story. Brad certainly wouldn't have asked me to do that—that wasn't like him—but I did feel the need to hang on and not let his story slip by, collecting dust in the archives.

There was more to it than that even. I felt somebody else prodding me. I felt it then, sitting in my chair staring at my computer screen, Brad's obituary glowing in front of me. I didn't hear a booming voice from above say, *Write the chapter; tell Brad's story.* But I did hear a voice.

It finally occurred to me it was Brad's voice. I saw him in my mind, that twinkle in his eye, and heard him talking in his relaxed way—although the words belonged to somebody else: "Be concerned not, I will be with you always." I once again saw him look past me out the window and heard him repeat the words. "Be concerned not, I will be with you always." Then he turned back to me with his playful smile.

"Now that's a heck of a message."

ESSAY
The Guard

"I heard the voice of God, and it saved my life."

He was a tall, lanky man with gray hair and a checked shirt, and I saw him ambling in my direction. I'd been busy signing books as a vendor at a small-town street festival and had the feeling folks were surprised a fella from Raleigh TV had come to spend a Saturday camped along their hometown curb. The town was Black Creek, and when the temperature that May afternoon hit ninety I found myself with a rare lull and figured the book buyers must have scrambled for the drink vendor. In fact, it had been the only time that day I didn't have a book to sign or someone to greet—until the lanky man approached.

He smiled and shook my hand and said he'd seen me on TV, said his name was Royce, Royce Pittman. He hooked his thumbs to his pockets and stole a glance at the sun. "Hot," he drawled, then looked down and studied my table.

He poked at my books, which I'd arranged in several neat piles. To fill the time and nudge a sale I explained I'd written two books about my TV travels. He merely hummed, and so I mentioned I was hard at work on a third. "But that one's a little different," I said.

"Yeah?"

"It's a book about miracles."

He looked at me. "Oh?"

I dove in, spilled the story of the golf broadcaster who told me about his long career, and who at the end said, "Oh, and by the way, I died and came back to life." I laughed at the punch line.

Royce didn't, and I saw the wrinkles tighten around his eyes; he squinted—though maybe not from the sun. He leaned on the table, his hand resting on one of my neat piles, but I was pretty sure he wasn't interested in my books; at least, not those I'd brought to the curb.

"I have heard the voice of God," he said. "And it saved my life."

His words struck me: the serious way he said them did, too. My mind jumped to my half-written manuscript again, in need of more material. I asked Royce if he'd mind waiting a second and turned to snatch a pen and pad from my backpack. "Go ahead," I told him.

"I was working in the backyard cutting briars, using a hand-held weed eater, and the cable wouldn't cut 'em. They were too tough. I went to change the head from string to a metal blade, a four-sided blade that was very sharp, and in order to put the blade on I had to take the guard off. So I took it off and thought to myself, *I don't need this guard. All I'm gonna do is cut some briars.* I was trying to convince myself I didn't need the guard. I just left it off.

"Anyway, I turned from the work bench with the weed eater in my hand, and when I got about twenty feet, a voice told me, 'Go back and put the guard on.' It was very distinct.

Well, I stopped in my tracks and thought, *Who is this who's just spoken to me? Is it my imagination?* But it was very distinct: 'Go back and put the guard on.' So I just stopped there for a few seconds thinking, then I told myself, *Oh, it's nothing,* and I walked to the door. And when I started out the door the voice said, 'Go back and put the guard on.' Very distinctly. And this time I got the message. I turned and went back to the work bench and put the guard on."

I was fairly certain I knew where Royce's story was headed, but that didn't lessen the tension, and tension is genuinely what I felt standing at the curb on that little town's central street in the middle of the day. It was the kind of hair prickling reserved for midnight ghost stories or whodunits. Royce could just as well have been talking about gripping a Smith and Wesson and steeling upon a masked intruder. A cranky weed eater and stubborn briars had the same effect.

"I walked to a tree with briars around it and revved the motor to where the blade was spinning real fast and the first swipe I took, the blade hit the tree and the machine jumped back and caught me right above my ankle. It hit hard enough to hurt, and the guard is the only thing that kept it from cutting my leg. There was no one home but me, and if it had cut my leg off, I probably would have bled to death." He nodded at me as if sure that's what would have happened.

I nodded back, impressed by the power of his simple story. There was no dying and coming back to life this time, just a little vignette about something people do all the time: cut briars with a weed eater. But would it really have cut off his leg? Would he truly have bled to death? I had my doubts, and maybe I should have followed up. Or maybe those questions were beside the point, because a peculiar irony came to me as well, complete with its own hair-prickling twist: I realized I had far more trouble with the weed eater than I did with the voice.

"This is a real story and not a figment of my imagination," Royce said. "I think about it all the time. I believe it was the voice of God."

That I could believe, too.

ALAN AND MARY WHANGER
The Shroud

I WAS AWARE OF THE MAN before anyone mentioned him, was conscious of him bent forward, arms planted on the table. I knew he had something to say before he said it.

We were in the fellowship room at a church in Durham. I'd been invited to talk about my television travels, but before the speech came lunch and I'd picked one of the round tables at random.

"You heard of the Shroud of Turin?" he said soon after I'd sat and muttered "nice-to-meet-you" to the others. He had a round face, gray hair and glasses, and wore a blue button-down open at the collar shirt beneath his tweed sport coat.

"Alan Whanger," he said and told me he was professor emeritus from Duke University Medical Center. He also explained his keen interest in the Shroud, which he'd been studying for more than thirty years. I watched him reach inside his coat pocket and figured he was fishing for a business card, but instead he pulled out a cellophane packet the size of a business envelope.

He opened the crinkly end and gave it a shake and out tumbled several pictures printed on what looked like index cards. He slid one to me, and when I looked down, my polite smile vanished. I was staring at the face of Jesus, a big charcoal close up, an in-your-face face, more haunting than holy. "The Shroud of Turin," Alan said. "The burial cloth of Jesus."

This was not the Jesus I'd seen in church. He looked much older and more hardened, ragged, his long hair stringy and disheveled, and his eyes clamped shut. I wasn't sure how to respond, but then Alan slid me another card and pointed, and now I nearly gasped.

In the picture before me stood a naked man, a full-frontal: Bare feet and skinny legs. And then my gaze traveled up the legs to—*Whoa!* Clasped hands covered a key part below the waist, the way I would do if a stranger barged in after I'd stepped from the shower. I hated to stare and jumped past the crossed hands, up the bare chest to the face. Jesus again. Naked Jesus.

What to say now? Fortunately, Alan started talking and rather fast. He explained that when Jesus died his followers wrapped the body in a linen sheet. I was familiar with the Shroud of Turin but knew more about the story of rolling a boulder in front of the tomb and three days later finding it shoved aside and the body gone, Jesus resurrected.

"But the linen cloth," Alan said. He told me it was still in the tomb, and when the people held it up they were amazed at what they saw. "They didn't have Jesus but they had his image, left by Jesus as evidence."

I wanted to ask how that was possible—Jesus leaving a detailed print of his body?—but somebody shouted that lunch was ready, come and get it, and the others began shooing me up. "Lead the way. You're the guest. You first."

I wished I could have asked Alan more. Easter was approaching, and I began to think the Shroud might make for a timely story. I did get a chance to ask him for another card before heading to the buffet. That one had his phone number.

*

Two weeks later, Alan met Robert and me at the front door of his retirement community. He shuffled his feet and patted his hips. "All set?" I think he and I both felt a little awkward, neither of us knowing what to expect. If he was anxious about the camera, I was equally anxious about the Shroud.

We rode the elevator to an upper floor, and once inside his apartment I immediately noticed the same photos he'd shown me at the luncheon, though dramatically enlarged on poster boards propped on easels around the far end of the room. The black-and-white images were striking—the front and back views of the body and that enormous face, so brooding and haunting. I peeled my eyes away only when Alan's wife entered. She couldn't have stood five-feet tall and might have been closer to four feet because of her bad back. She was bent forward and likely weighed less than a hundred pounds. Alan introduced me to Mary, and she extended her hand and welcomed me with a soft voice.

I could tell Robert was excited about the dramatic poster-board pictures. *His* face seemed large, too, or at least his eyes, and he scrambled about, setting up his camera and a light. We started rolling five minutes after entering.

"This is the face on the Shroud of Turin," Alan said, "probably the best known face in human existence." He pointed, nearly tapping Jesus on the nose. "The nose is dislocated right here, and there's actually a depression across the cheek. He was obviously struck across the face with a stick of some sort. And we can see down here, part of the beard has been pulled out."

It wasn't a full beard but more like a cotton tuft, which on closer inspection looked uneven. "Someone grabbed the beard and just pulled." Alan yanked down, mimicking the act. "It's a sign of ultimate mockery if you pull a fella's beard out."

He moved to the next oversized photo, which showed the back of the body. "And here we see the unbraided ponytail he was wearing as many Jews did at the time."

Jesus in a ponytail? I thought. I couldn't recall ever seeing him in a ponytail.

"We can see these contusions across the shoulder in a pattern where the tissue has been squashed down, and so logically he was carrying something across his shoulders. And here we can see he was literally hit from head to foot by a terrible Roman scourge."

Alan described the scourge as a Roman whip with metal barbs on the end.

"So every time he was hit, it would drive the barbs in, and when pulled, it would tear little bits of flesh out. He was hit at least 125 times, front and back. Just turned into a bloody mass. This is a powerful image."

"You're not kidding," I managed. It made it all seem real, too real—and too graphic for my television story. I suggested we sit for the rest of the interview.

Alan told me he first learned of the Shroud in 1977 when he and Mary stopped at a bookstore in Chapel Hill. "And I saw this book."

He turned and asked Mary to bring it to him, and I watched her shuffle across the room, bent forward, and return with the paperback. Alan held it up and there was that brooding face again. "That's the first time I'd ever seen that image," he said.

He became more fascinated later when a colleague showed him a rare image of Jesus supposedly copied from the Shroud in the year A.D. 550. "If we could prove that," Alan said, "then the Shroud would have to be at least dated to the sixth century." Such proof would lend it authenticity and disprove claims it was a much later forgery.

Photography happened to be Alan's lifelong hobby, and he set about inventing a photographic technique that showed multiple "points of congruence" between the two images. The discovery was a breakthrough and earned him international recognition.

So I wasn't surprised when Alan told me he'd seen the Shroud in person. The sacred cloth is locked in a cathedral in Turin, Italy, kept secure under glass.

"You've seen it through the glass?" I asked.

"No," he said. "I've seen it without the glass."

That response did surprise me.

"Oh, yes. I've been one foot from the Shroud."

Alan told me his photographic analysis showed that Jesus had been wrapped in the cloth along with the nails that held him to the cross, the hammer used to pound them in and pliers for wrenching them out, plus a Roman spear and two scourges.

I listened, fascinated by the evidence, because if what Alan said was true then it was likely all true, everything I'd heard in church about the crucifixion—and possibly the resurrection.

It wasn't just faith and air anymore but real and tangible, splayed out in physical form on the Shroud.

"Do you feel you have helped prove the existence of Jesus?"

"Well, we think that's what the Shroud does."

He credited his wife for her invaluable help and turned several times to ask Mary for certain documents. I watched her again walk slowly back and forth across the room and began to worry about the time. I was gathering more information than I probably needed, and yet my gut told me something was missing. What seemed to be missing was Jesus.

That's who we were talking about: Jesus at the time of his death. Jesus, Lord and Savior, lost to man. But where was the emotion? My gut screamed—and so did my back. I looked at Mary.

Alan had often used the word "we." He'd say, "We discovered…" The two had authored a book together on the Shroud with Alan handling much of the research and Mary most of the writing.

I interrupted to ask Mary if I could interview her, which seemed to come as a surprise to both of them. "Well, I guess so," Alan said, and Mary said the same.

She wore a red dress and had clipped a barrette on one side of her short dark hair. I think of teenage girls wearing barrettes. Mary said she was 86, a year older than Alan, but to me there was an almost childlike innocence about her. She was nearly child sized, very petite, and seemed helpful and kind, like a gentle soul who spoke softly and listened well.

"We didn't have any opinion in the beginning as to whether the Shroud was authentic or not," she began. "I'm not a scientist, so Alan had to figure out how to do the research.

But I did help him all along the way, and as we got involved I became more and more fascinated."

"Why?" I asked.

"Well, I've been a Christian for as long as I can remember." She paused and seemed to gather her thoughts before speaking again. "People wear—and I do, too—decorative crosses, and it all looks so beautiful and clean."

Maybe I was just seeing what I wanted to see, but her eyes appeared moist.

"It wasn't clean, and it wasn't beautiful. It was horrible what Jesus went through. And for me as a Christian, it helps me understand better than ever before how much he loved all of us, even me, to willingly go through that suffering and that kind of death."

She too had seen the Shroud at the cathedral in Turin. "It was rather overwhelming," she said. "My eyes were just drawn to that face. Looking at the evidence of all the wounds, the scourging and bruising and everything else he went through, that hurts."

"I mean, it really brings it to life," I said.

"It does bring it to life."

"And death?"

"And death."

I admit I led her with that last exchange. I'd been looking for a way to close my story, and she had delivered—the life-and-death line made for a clean ending. The interview was over. I had what I needed.

"And this has nothing really to do with what we've been talking about, but in a way it confirms it for me," she began just as I was about to rise from the table. It startled me a bit, her talking again since the comment before had seemed like the natural end to our conversation. "Because this shows to me, this shows the resurrection, which means life goes on." I wasn't sure what she was getting at but nodded, hoping this was just a brief interlude before I could thank her and get up.

"Well..." she said, and once again I sensed she was searching for the right words. "I had a near-death experience back in 2005. I didn't see anybody or anything, but I found myself suspended between this world and the next, and I can't tell you how I knew that, but that's what it seemed to me. I was very sick at the time. There was no interval. I was lying in bed sick, and then all at once I wasn't there anymore. I was between."

I almost couldn't believe what I was hearing. Did she know I was writing a book about miracles? I felt something half divine happen at that moment, there at that table, with Jesus close by on the poster boards.

"A little while later—I have no idea how long; I don't think very long—I was back in bed, sick. But there was nothing except peace I felt during that experience. And these two things for me—what we see on the Shroud and that experience—tie together to help me not worry at all about death."

She spoke gently but with such certainty, and for me those two things tied together, too. She was so small and nonthreatening, vulnerable and therefore believable. I believed her. It was hard not to.

"I haven't told this to many people," she said and mentioned the obvious contrast between Alan's scientific research and her other-world experience and implied how one might undermine the other. When I asked how many people she had told, she said, "Only a handful."

Now I did feel a great sense of something important happening, and her statement begged a question. "Well, why are you telling me?"

She looked down, and I knew she was wrestling with her response, wanting it to come out right. When she finally did reply, her three short words were so utterly simple and yet so profoundly complex.

"I don't know," she said.

And that's all she said. Somehow she didn't need to say more.

*

I was back in the Whanger's apartment several weeks later and this time had come alone, though once again with a camera, the little camcorder type, which would help me document Mary's story for my book. There was so much more I wanted to ask.

We sat at the same small table where I'd interviewed them before, and that action itself set the tone. I had come for Mary's story, but Alan took a chair, too, and I welcomed his presence—anything to make Mary feel at ease in sharing her near-death drama.

"It started with a toothache."

I wondered if I'd heard correctly. *A toothache? Where was the drama in that?*

"I've never had much problem with my teeth, so it really took me by surprise."

She told me it was September 2005 when she and Alan were headed to Dallas for an international Shroud conference. She saw her dentist before she left; he discovered the beginnings of an abscess and prescribed an antibiotic. During the trip a second tooth began to ache, so she contacted her dentist again who urged her to keep taking the antibiotic.

"In fact, I thought it was better," Mary said, "because by the time we came back home I was not having any pain with either tooth, and I didn't feel sick in any way. I just felt exceedingly tired."

She went to bed that night, while Alan stayed up. He often spent nights on Shroud research, working and sleeping downstairs.

"Well, about five the next morning I woke up so sick I could barely get out of bed." She struggled to the bathroom and back but didn't have the energy to call downstairs for Alan. "I soon realized I was so sick that if I went to sleep I might not wake up, so I decided I would try to stay awake until Alan came upstairs, hoping he might be able to do something to help me feel better."

"She was extremely ill," Alan said. "I was sure that one of her abscesses had ruptured into her bloodstream to cause this acute, severe illness."

"Is that what happened? The abscess ruptured into her bloodstream?"

"That's almost certainly what happened because she had two dental abscesses." He mentioned blood poisoning, and now I understood—the term itself sounded frightening. "Obviously something drastic had happened, and I wanted to get her to the emergency room as fast as I could."

"I remember when we entered the emergency room," Mary said. "The security person was sitting by the entry door and took one look at me and waved us in without asking any questions. I must have really looked ill."

At some point during the crisis Mary managed to tell Alan the fear she'd had about falling asleep and never waking up. "What I was not able to tell Alan was the near-death experience I had."

This is what I had come for, and once again I was glad Alan was here, hoping he might connect the Shroud to Mary's near-death experience. Somehow I felt there *was* a connection.

The oversized pictures of Jesus weren't propped around the room anymore. They'd been taken down, the easels folded up, but on my second visit to this apartment I still sensed the Shroud's presence. Jesus had been nailed to the cross and left for dead—and his pictures probably stored in the Whanger's hall closet—but I felt he was still close, hovering near this very table.

"All at once I felt myself suspended," Mary began. "That's the best word I have ever come up with—suspended between this world and the next. I realized I was not asleep, I was not dreaming, it was not a hallucination, and I can't tell you how I knew that, but I just knew.

"I wasn't upset by all this. I was very calm, and I stayed calm all through the experience. It was not a dramatic experience. I didn't see Jesus or anyone else. I was just in this space. I felt myself not very far from the world and yet completely cut off from it."

As I listened to Mary, I felt myself caught between two different places. I was intrigued but at the same time disheartened. "You didn't see *anything?*"

"No, I didn't. That's the strange part to me. I mean, you look at the sky and it's this huge thing. Well, I didn't feel I was in a huge place. I felt like I was—I don't know—I use the word suspended. I was just all of a sudden in this place, and I felt it was probably high and deep but not very wide. I sort of was enclosed, but not like being in… Here's where words get difficult—not like being in a room. It happened quickly and with absolutely no loss of mind or awareness, as if I were standing just this side of that doorway and stepped inside."

I thought of the closet door. *Was Jesus in there?* I asked again if she was sure. "You didn't see anything?"

"No. I didn't see any bright colors or lights. If there was any color at all I'd say it was gray. It just seemed gray everywhere."

"So you did see gray? Or is seeing the right word?"

"I don't know. I think maybe I felt it more than saw it. But the thing that impressed me so much was my complete separation from anywhere other than the space where I was. I had absolutely no contact with earth or with another world. I was just between, but I was not anxious or afraid. I had the greatest sense of peace.

"Some people say something about your life flashes before you. That didn't happen. I did, though, think of things I was trying to get done that I didn't want to leave for somebody else to do. Alan and I have always had a busy life, and I work best when there's order around me. It doesn't bother Alan how high things pile up. Somebody told him once there are filers and pilers. Well, he's definitely a piler."

They both laughed.

"Fortunately, I married a filer," Alan said.

"I did not hear a voice, but I did get a message," Mary continued. "It wasn't spoken but it was clear, as if it had been spoken, telling me it's okay. I mean, I'm not using the right words; I doubt God used the word 'okay'—although I guess he could have if he wanted. But I felt peace. Somebody else would take care of what needed to be taken care of. That to me was probably the most amazing thing about the experience, is the complete feeling of peace I had."

She couldn't say how long she was in this other place or even how she returned.

"Just all of a sudden I felt myself back in bed."

"I mean, did you open your eyes?"

"I guess. I know I was still at peace." Her fingers played with the tabletop. "It was such a deep experience, so profoundly moving to me, and as I mentioned earlier I couldn't tell anybody for three months. I couldn't find the right words. It would have been like trying to describe a gorgeous sunrise or sunset to a blind person who'd always been blind and had never seen any color. There just aren't words."

She told me about Christmas that year, 2005, when she and Alan planned to visit their daughter and her family in Connecticut. "We were going to leave the next morning, and the evening before I took a shower and washed my hair, and in the process of drying my hair I saw I had more gray than I'd ever noticed before. For some reason that released me and I was able to talk about the experience. It connected in some way and let me feel free to talk about it."

To me, the connection seemed a bit random.

"It does to me, too," she said and nodded at Alan. "This is the psychiatrist over here. See if he can come up with something."

We'd been ignoring Alan, and I was glad to welcome him back.

"I think seeing the gray hair indicated her time was limited," he said, which seemed an obvious conclusion once he'd said it. "She had something very important to share, and it was the time to bring it out. It's a powerful personal experience and obviously, I, as her husband, am very concerned about these sorts of things and highly interested in spiritual matters, too. I have dealt with a lot of dying people, and I know profound things can happen at those times."

His answer surprised me. "But being a doctor, you probably come from more of a science background," I said. "So was it hard for you to grasp this out-of-body experience? Does it go against the grain of your scientific training?"

"Not particularly. I've had some experiences myself, reviving the dead, and that sort of thing."

That answer came as a greater surprise.

"I went to undergrad at Duke," he began, "and then medical school and took a residency in psychiatry and a fellowship in geriatric psychiatry and then joined the faculty." He launched into his long background. "I'm trained in general surgery and tropical medicine. We were missionaries in what is now Zimbabwe."

I had a feeling Zimbabwe is where this was headed.

"We had a 200-bed hospital and treated almost anything that came in: ruptured pregnancies, broken limbs, animal bites, Machete slashes." He chuckled, then shifted and rested his arms on the table.

"I remember a patient I had, a woman I guess in her mid-thirties, extremely ill. We operated and she was just filled with cancer, an abdomen full of masses, and we couldn't do anything other than take a little biopsy. The next day the nurse came up and said the lady had just died, so I went down to see her and, indeed, she had no pulse and was quite dead. I guess a little compulsively I did CPR on her, and fairly soon she started to breath and opened her eyes. Then she smiled a very beatific smile, and I never will forget, she said, 'Zvakanaka, Chiremba. Ndinofara, ndinofara,' which means, 'It is well, doctor. I am happy. I am happy.' So it was kind of a profound thing, her reaction. She died shortly thereafter, and I didn't try to revive her again." He smiled. "I said, 'Well, this lady, she's ready to go, and I'm not gonna drag her back.'"

I was gaining a new perspective on Alan. He had a resume piled with credentials, but I think he also had a nose for storytelling.

"I don't want to get too far off track," he said, "but after we'd been in the mission hospital for a year and a half some of us thought, 'We really ought to have some sort of prayer service or something.'

"Well, I had a forty-bed unit of male tuberculosis patients and a semi-retired pastor there who had a massive lung abscess from the TB. He was dying, and we moved him to a small private room so his family could be with him. This was on a night we were having our healing service, and of course we prayed for him. But the next morning when I went to his room, there he was sitting up on the side of the bed smiling, and he was feeling remarkably well for having practically been dead the night before. But anyway, his lung abscess cleared up very quickly and his liver started functioning again, and two weeks later he came to our healing service and delivered the message. That sort of convinced a number of people that there was something going on here."

Alan said the pastor was sixty-eight at the time and served thirteen rural churches and was soon on the circuit again, making the rounds on a bicycle, which he pedaled until he was seventy. Then he became the hospital chaplain for several years more. "And obviously he had a very strong interest in patients," Alan added with a laugh.

The miracles were suddenly piling up—Alan really was a piler—and it occurred to me that maybe I'd been part of a miracle myself. I asked Mary about the last time we'd sat at this table, when she'd spoken of her near-death experience. "You said you hadn't told many people. I was kind of surprised you told me all of a sudden."

"Well, I was surprised, too," she said "because I hadn't really thought about it in advance. I think the Lord gave me the urge to do it, and I don't know how to say that any differently, either. I don't hear voices, but occasionally I have heard—well, not heard. 'Heard' I guess is not the right word, but there has seemed to be communication that has somehow come to me as though it were words. Not very often."

She said she'd told her near-death experience to about ten people.

"I don't tell it unless I feel an urgency, and people I've told it to have seemed grateful."

I counted myself one of those grateful people. How could she have known I was writing a book about people who'd experienced miracles? I considered it a small miracle, the miracle she'd given me.

Back then I had come for a story on the Shroud, which was part of my visit this time, too. I felt Mary's miracle and Jesus' cloth could not be separated. I felt Alan couldn't be separated, either. He was part of the conversation.

"*The Scientific Disproval of God*," he announced. It was the name of the book he'd written when he was fifteen and that he later ended up burning. "I finally decided I couldn't disprove him, so I better join him," he said, chuckling.

That fascinated me—Alan trying at first to disprove God with science, and then using science to prove the reality of God's sacred cloth. He seemed a man full of contradictions, yet his science and his faith had somehow come to complement one another.

While studying medicine at Duke, he began to think about meeting the right woman. "Better marry somebody who could put up with me." He was thinking that very thought the night of a campus pep rally. "I started praying the right woman would show up. Then the door opened." It was the entrance to one of the buildings. "And here this lady stood, and she had a light behind her head. It wasn't a divine halo, just some light in the hallway, but as soon as I saw her I thought, *That's the one.*" It was Mary, a Duke undergrad and Religion major.

"Even having graduated from Duke four times, I'd never heard of the Shroud," Alan said. Not until he and Mary were in that bookstore and he noticed the paperback with the strange face on the cover. Now they had become two of the world's leading Shroud scholars.

"There's a certain connection between the near death and the Shroud," Alan said, and I leaned in, for here finally was the longed-for connection.

"The Shroud shows Jesus having died and come back and confirms in a graphic way that this is not the end of things. It shows there is life after death because it shows the moment of resurrection. It illustrates an instantaneous transition from a material to a spiritual state, and Mary's experience was near that experience, but she came back."

At first, Mary had connected with the Shroud through her writings, but then came this deeper connection in which she seemed to have shared part of Jesus' journey, all the while wrapped completely in peace.

"It is an awesome thing to see," Alan said about the Shroud. He told me he'd seen it eight different times at the cathedral in Turin. "It puts the hair up in the back of my head, not from fear but awe. The face just has remarkable power, not the cloth but the image."

I asked whether his Shroud research had brought him closer to God.

"Oh, very much so. I've been one foot away from the Shroud. I've been looking straight into the face of Jesus on his burial cloth."

"I couldn't take my eyes away," Mary added. "It was a deeply moving experience. I just felt drawn to it, very worshipful, although I don't worship the cloth at all. People get upset sometimes because they think we're worshiping a cloth, which we don't. But the majesty of that face, even with the signs of suffering—I just couldn't take my eyes from the face image, from *his* eyes."

I asked them both—Mary at 86 and Alan at 85—whether they worried about approaching the end of their lives.

"I don't particularly worry about it," Alan said. "I think it's going to be very interesting." He laughed. "I'd rather it not be painful, but I'm ready to go at any time."

"*Where* do you think you'll go? How do you picture that?"

"Well, the Scripture speaks of a New Jerusalem, a locale with a structure to it and that the Lord is making provision for us and we'll go there when we die. I kind of anticipate what's called the Rapture, and the Lord is going to come back and take his people out when things are getting bad. They're going to get a whole lot worse for a while till he comes back and gets the whole mess straightened out." He laughed again before closing with a final thought, spoken not like a scientist but as a loving husband. "I'm just grateful the Lord has given me a wonderful wife to share these past sixty years."

By now, more than half a day had passed inside that small apartment, and I wasn't quite sure what I'd accomplished. Had I gained a better understanding of what happens when we die? Mary's experience lacked any kind of big reveal—all she saw, or felt, was gray—but somehow I did feel closer to knowing what happens. Although I supposed that didn't make much sense, because how can anyone understand death if they haven't died? Near-death only comes close.

But maybe I had accomplished something. Jesus might have been tucked in the Whanger's hall closet, but I did think maybe I'd pried the door a crack. As for Mary, well, she'd apparently taken a whole step inside.

"I'm not eager to die, but I'm not afraid of it," she said in her soft voice. "I am very comforted to know that when I do make that transition there will be no loss of awareness, at least I don't feel there will be. I mean I obviously didn't go ahead and finish dying, but it was such a comforting, peaceful experience."

She tried to elaborate, grappled with the right words, used the term "awesome," which struck me as funny—someone 86 years old speaking the lingo of my teenage son. She was actually using it to describe both her near-death experience and the Shroud of Turin, and on second thought, maybe that was as close a description as anyone could ever get.

We were done at the table. The interview was over, and I closed my pad, rose from my seat and thanked them both, and they thanked me. There was no awkwardness anymore; that feeling had long since vanished. In fact, I felt like hugging them—but didn't. Well, maybe there was some lingering awkwardness. I wasn't sure if reporters hug researchers or vice versa. A sincere thank you was enough.

Because I *was* sure of one thing when I turned and left that apartment— or rather, two things. I was sure I had become closer to them.

And through them, I had become closer to the man on the cloth.

MILLIE
Little Angels

"I'M A HILLBILLY FROM WAY BACK," Millie said, and I sat there thinking she was right. But also wrong.

She was big boned, favored short-sleeve shirts that flaunted her thick arms, and her speech was Southern twangy. "I love country music, but the country music today is not pretty like it used to be." I noticed she said "is not pretty" instead of "ain't pretty" or "ain't purdy."

Her dark eyes slid from mine and her head rolled to the pillow's center. "I went to see the Grand Ole Opry in 1982 and again in '91 or '92, I think, and thoroughly enjoyed it." I wondered what country star she might be seeing on the ceiling.

Millie was my grandmother's best friend from across the street. I'd known her my whole life and had kept in touch even after Grandmommy's death, but I had rarely stepped inside Millie's house and certainly never before in her bedroom. It was a big bedroom with yellow walls and a bare floor and wide space between where I sat against the wall and where Millie lay beneath the covers. Pill bottles crowded her nightstand, except for a tissue box that hogged half of it. An oxygen machine squatted by the bed, its springy tubes hanging limp,

146

and I assumed she must be having a good day since she wasn't using it.

"The nurse's aide bathed me just for you."

"Oh," I said. "Well, you look good."

She did look good; in fact, she looked like she always had—her hair cut short with bangs and not a single strand of gray, totally black. She'd probably dyed it for years, but still, Millie never seemed old to me, even though she was in her eighties now.

I was glad I'd made the three-hour drive from Raleigh to Richmond to see her. I'd brought my son along, telling him he could skip school and thinking it might be fun for the two of us to drive up, see Grandmommy's old house, knock on the door, and ask the new owners if they'd mind letting us look around, and of course visit with Millie before going someplace fun for a late lunch.

It was raining when we turned onto Dorchester and rolled past all the brick houses nestled close to one another. I drove slowly and thought back to spring breaks I'd spent at Grandmommy's when the dogwoods and azaleas were in bloom and the street was like a fluffy pillow of pink and white and the air smelled of warm honey. I breathed in, but today it smelled like wet bark.

Millie's was another brick house, a simple one with a flat front, minus angles or dormers or any architectural doo dads. I hugged the curb and thought how strange it was parking there instead of across the street.

I looked over at 5404, the number still on Grandmommy's light post at the sidewalk. The front lawn had been cut, even groomed at the edges, and I was glad the new owners had kept the house's pale-green trim. Or were they new owners? How many times had the house changed hands? Grandmommy had been gone almost fifteen years now and Granddaddy more than twenty. They'd spent most of their lives in the little two-story brick, which did include dormer windows, plus a walkway dividing the lawn into equal squares. The brick walk had been my fifty-yard line whenever I tossed the Nerf football as a kid. I smiled at the memory and traced the walkway to the stoop till my gaze came to the front door, and then I frowned. The door was red. Grandmommy's had been hunter green.

I told my son Scout we'd give a knock when we left Millie's, that maybe the rain would quit by then so we wouldn't get soaked waiting for strangers to open their red door. It was coming down pretty hard and we waited a minute even before jumping out and running up the steps to Millie's. So I kept looking at Grandmommy's. And I saw Millie again.

I saw her through the slats of Grandmommy's blinds, marching across the street, head bent, full steam. "Millie's coming!" I used to shout to the house. Millie walked like she had water boiling on the stove and needed teabags. Or she could have just wanted to pass the time. She bulled ahead either way, and I worried about cars. Millie walking with her head down like that, not bothering to look. Dorchester Road was sometimes busy, and that wasn't the worst of it. Millie was blind.

"Blind, poo," Grandmommy would say. She'd sneak up behind me and peer through the slats herself. *Poo* was a Grandmommy-ism. "Blind, my foot." *My foot* was, too.

"She told you like it was," Millie said and rolled her head back across the pillow and pointed her dark eyes somewhere near mine. "In a lot of ways she was like a mother to me, more than my own mother. I left home when I was eighteen, and I knew her since I was nineteen. She always used to tell me how huge I was." I winced. "She did, little Scotty, and you know she did." Millie called me little Scotty, my dad big Scotty.

I knew what Millie meant and could hear Grandmommy even now. *Poo!* But I could also see Grandmommy sitting in the living room—painted pale-green, too—on the edge of her cushiony wingback chair, bouncing her bad leg on the footrest and laughing with Millie over something or other.

"There wasn't anything I wouldn't do for her, and there wasn't anything she wouldn't do for me." I was glad Millie was talking about Grandmommy now, though it felt like a talk tinged with finality. Why *was* Millie talking about this now?

"She was real sick, little Scotty, and I called your momma and told her she should be at the hospital, and the last thing your grandmomma said was, 'Where is Millie?'"

I hadn't known that, hadn't known much about Grandmommy dying at all, which made me think of the one time I had heard her mention death. She'd been stretched on the den couch, which had doubled as her bed when she couldn't climb the stairs anymore. The TV was on, and maybe it was something we were watching that prompted her to tell me she was afraid to die. She just out and said it. I never said anything back.

"She gave me her rings when she was in the hospital 'cause they were so loose," Millie said, "and she gave me her rings to give to your momma. She and your granddaddy were one of the sweetest couples you ever wanted to meet and did anything for anybody."

Scout hadn't known either one of them, and I was glad he'd come with me and hoped he was listening. I'm sure he was happy to miss school, though he probably wished he could have skipped the collared shirt and khaki pants. He sat quietly against the other wall, fingers linked in his lap.

I asked Millie if she'd mind if I took notes, not knowing whether that was proper etiquette, but she said sure, and the way she said it made me think she even felt honored. If this really was the last time I'd see Millie, then I wanted to keep something of her, even if it was just words. I had the feeling words might be more valuable than rings.

"I grew up in Bedford County," she said and looked at the ceiling again, which I guessed she couldn't see. "I came to Richmond in 1951 to study, went to school to be a beautician. In 1953, I earned thirty dollars a week as a beautician at Thalhimer's. I did a lot of it by feel. My customers didn't know I was blind. One time a New York hair stylist said, 'That one there has the most sensitive touch I've ever seen.'" Millie let out a sigh—a satisfied one, I thought.

She told me she lived at the Y and met Elmer Ernest when she was twenty-two. He'd been introduced to the lady across the hall, and they double dated, and Millie ended up with Elmer Ernest. She called him Rusty, and they were married April 30, 1955. He drove a Trailways bus, and in 1958 they had a son, Richard.

In fact, it was Richard who'd opened Millie's front door and shown Scout and me to the back bedroom, which felt strange. All those holidays I'd spent at Grandmommy's, and I'd seen

Richard only a couple of times. Now he was in his mid-fifties, clad in jeans and a denim shirt, wearing a ponytail and waving us in. Millie's house was dark and gloomy, the blinds clamped shut. The floors creaked, and everything smelled like chicken. We followed Richard past the sparse living room, and I asked how his mom was doing, keeping my voice down. "Well..." he said, and nothing more, and then we were in the bedroom, which was surprisingly bright. The lights were on.

I walked over to Millie, leaned across the bed, and gave her a hug; she propped herself as best she could to give Scout one, too. When I turned around, Richard was gone.

"I've got the most wonderful son anybody's ever had. He's taken care of me like a baby, more than most men would do for their wives."

She told me about moving to Dorchester Road in 1964, developing blood clots in 1978, twice in her lungs and once in her right arm, which she lost use of for a while. Then Rusty died in 1980. "He had cancer all over his body." I would have been eighteen then but never knew Rusty, or at least didn't remember him.

"My stomach was bothering me so bad," she said of her own cancer diagnosis in January, 2012. She took chemo pills, but less than two years later, "the whole right side of my heart was gone." She'd been in and out of the hospital ever since, including just a week ago. "I was so full of fluid, I couldn't breathe. I was just sick all over."

But she didn't look that sick. *My foot!* Maybe she was just having one of her good days. Maybe I *would* see her again sometime—or maybe not. In any case, I had learned from letting too many past opportunities slip away, and so I grabbed my chance to write down Millie's thoughts.

"A blind person's life is not as sad as what a lot of people think it is. It's really what you make it. For instance, I could knit—caps, coats, blankets—and not everybody can do that."

She told me how she used to bring homemade cookies to prison inmates and talked about bowling with her blind friends each week, and I nodded because I'd once done a story on blind bowling and knew how it worked. The bowlers used bumpers along the lanes to avoid gutter balls.

She talked about all the years she volunteered at the home for the blind. "I scrubbed floors, did laundry, made up beds. I was just an all-around helper. The happiest thing in my life was being able to help someone else—not think of yourself but someone else."

I asked about getting around, going to the store, running errands, and she admitted that had been a handicap, not being able to drive or take care of the yard. "A doctor friend who's retired does the weeding. He's gonna be one of the pallbearers." She meant one of *her* pallbearers.

I brought up dying and once again surprised myself. It was an awfully blunt question, asking what she thought, but I found I'd grown tired of bumpers, of playing it safe, and in a way it seemed natural given the circumstances. It was a question I'd failed to ask my own grandmother.

"I feel like I have lived a good, clean, Christian life, the way God wanted me to live, and I feel like I'm ready to die. Of course, that's something no one knows how long it'll be." She turned her head to the ceiling again. "I would love to have seen the Christmas lights at the Botanical Gardens."

I surprised myself once more, this time by not asking a question at all and just letting the moment sit, waiting for Millie to fill it.

"Back in the 70s my sister had cancer." She said she visited her sister's bedside one day and was leaving the hospital, walking down the corridor. "And I actually felt someone tap me on the shoulder and say, 'You'll never see her again.' It was an actual voice." Her sister died soon after.

"There have been other times I've heard voices." I thought Millie would elaborate, but instead she moved on. "The other night a friend was holding my hand on one side of the bed, and I felt someone holding my other hand. But there was no one there."

She paused another moment before speaking again. "I'm happy. I feel like I'm going to be in a better place. I look forward to seeing Momma and Daddy and just all the little angels flying around and being happy together. You just think about God and all his angels." She seemed sure the little angels had wings and described streets paved in gold. I thought of the Wizard of Oz—I couldn't help it—and chided myself for picturing heaven as a make-believe fairyland.

She turned her head to me again. "I'm tired, but, Scotty, you'll never know how much it means for me to see you."

Her energy seemed to be flagging, and so I stood, bridged the wide space between us, bent and gave her a hug, and she hugged back with surprising strength. Scout walked over and gave her a hug, too. "Scout, you were as quiet today as you were as a baby," she said, and I caught him smiling. He told her it was nice seeing her, and then we both made our way to the other side again, stopping at the bedroom door to turn and say goodbye one last time.

That was the moment, the one more than any other that lasts for me, when I saw Millie's face from across the room. Her eyes were fixed to the floor or wall or some other place, and I noticed just how dark the circles were under her eyes. I wondered what she was seeing, and I let that moment sit, too, waiting for Millie—or someone—to fill it.

I didn't feel a tap on my shoulder or hear a voice in my ear, but I think I knew. And yet I told myself I would see Millie again. I even told that to Millie. "I'll try to come back soon," I said, my tone full of upbeat optimism. She was strong; she didn't look that sick. She'd hang in, I thought.

"Bye, Millie," I said, but she didn't respond. Her face remained blank, and the image imprinted itself in my mind. I had the sense that when I left, a part of my life would leave. I'm certain Millie knew this was it, too, which somehow made the link between us even stronger now that it was at the end. She may—or may not have been—legally blind, but there was no doubt Millie had always possessed keen insight.

It was still raining when Scout and I walked outside, even harder than it had been earlier, but we walked across the street anyway, and I rang Grandmommy's doorbell. I wondered if the plastic mat was still there, the gray one she'd kept on the other side of the door so that when people came in they wouldn't drag dirt on the carpet. That durned mat. Half the time I'd trip on it, and what was the point of keeping the carpet clean if you never laid eyes on it? How Grandmommy never tripped was beyond me. Instead, she'd hurt her leg missing a step on the way down to the basement. I found I'd also grown tired of plastic mats.

I thought again of watching Millie through the blinds, leaning awkwardly over Grandmommy's record player, which sat on a little peg-legged table just below the window. It must have played "Blue Christmas" by Elvis Presley a gazillion times. *Ba, ba, ba, bluuueee...* I sang the song in my head in front of the red door.

When no one answered I gave it a couple of loud knocks, knowing it was probably useless, but we stood on the stoop anyway while the time ticked and the rain fell. I bet we stood a good three or four minutes, but it didn't matter.

No one ever opened the door.

LAURA
My Sister

DEAR LAURA,

You may not know what happened to you—or maybe you do—but in case you don't, I thought I should explain. It happened so suddenly. One moment you were fine, and the next you were gone. I'm trying to make sense of it myself.

None of us had any idea what was coming, and I don't think you did, either. Ed says you'd been feeling tired that week, but it was nothing alarming. You probably don't even remember telling him that.

You may have also forgotten the date it happened. It's been a while now, but I remember and always will, and so will Mom and Dad, Ed and your kids. It was October 3, 2015.

You went shopping that day with Georgia, and I'm so glad you did. You spent your last full day with your daughter, which in retrospect seems like its own little miracle. Georgia had just started working at the ad agency, and I bet part of you wished she had ventured beyond Virginia Beach, taken a chance and looked for opportunities away from home. But what if she had? That day between you would have been lost— October 3rd, a mother-daughter day, as if it was meant to be.

Did the two of you listen to Lee's music in the car? He's still living in Nashville, and his band just released its first album. You would have been so proud and excited for him. I always felt the two of you shared a special bond, stronger than many mothers share with their sons.

I know you missed Lee, and Georgia, too, when she moved into her new apartment, although she hasn't lived there since it happened. She's back home keeping Ed company, and I understand they've had some good father-daughter talks. Losing you has been rough on them, but they're getting by. They have their jobs and friends and they're both back to playing tennis. Remember, that's one of the things you told Georgia that day. You said she should pick up her racquet again and not let her talent go to waste. She and Ed even played in a tournament together at the club. They won the consolation round.

Here I am telling you things that have happened since or that maybe you didn't remember before, and the irony is I'm the one who had the memory problem. I saw the neurologist on a Friday, and he asked what I was doing Monday. "Same surgery Peyton Manning had," he said. "Your spine." It sounded frightening, but then Peyton went back to leading the Broncos. You didn't get to see Denver win the Super Bowl.

After my surgery, you called me at the hospital, but I was on so much medication I barely remembered. When you called me at home four days later, on Friday, October 2nd, I woke up to my cell ringing. My head was heavy and I couldn't find the phone at first. When I finally did, I saw your name splayed across the screen in bright white letters—I remember that distinctly. I fumbled, trying to answer, but by the time I did you'd already hung up. I think I called you right back, but I'm not sure, and if I did call I can't remember our conversation. That would have been our last one. Forever.

So you and Georgia went shopping the next day, and there was the party that night at the club outside near the tennis courts. All your friends were there, the weather was warm, and Ed's band was playing.

Around 6:30 the band started in on a Led Zeppelin song, "D'yer Mak'er," a strange name and hard tune to dance to. You and a friend went to the restroom, and at one point you stood in front of the mirror, bowed and flicked your head back in order to fluff your hair, the way a lot of girls do. But the jerky motion made you dizzy. You said you felt "weird"—that's the word you used. "Must be that Oktoberfest beer," you said, though you'd had just one. "Guess I'm not used to it."

A moment later you exited and walked toward one of the food tables, probably thinking if you ate something you'd feel better. A friend was walking toward you and waved. "Hey, Laura," he said, but you didn't respond, which he thought was odd because you said hi to everybody. Then he noticed something odder still. You began to tilt and wobble out of his path, and he realized something was wrong. Your knees buckled, and he rushed toward you, caught you, and broke your fall. You slumped against him, and he settled you gently on the ground.

A few people noticed and weren't sure what was going on, only that someone was down in the middle of the party, in the middle of that Led Zeppelin song:

Oh, oh oh, oh oh, you don't have to go…

Then people realized it was you, which they thought unusual, you of all people lying flat on the stone patio. You were always full of energy and loved to dance. Many told me later they thought you were the best dancer they'd ever seen. The person who called 911 said your skin immediately turned gray. People crouched beside you and assumed you'd fainted. They kept saying, "Wake up, Laura, wake up," and rolled ice cubes on your face. Someone held your head in their lap. I'm sure you would have been embarrassed by all the attention, but there was nothing you could do. There was nothing anyone could do. You didn't move. Your eyes didn't twitch.

Oh oh, ay ay, baby please don't go.

A woman rushed up to Ed and shouted over the music. "Something's happened to Laura." Ed quit banging the drums and hustled over. He went to his knees and held your hand. "Laura," he called, and when there was no response he patted your face and called your name again. "Laura."

Oh oh, darling, please don't go.

The guitar player never saw Ed leave. He was concentrating on the song, which was especially tough to play, and suddenly the rhythm seemed off. He looked up and discovered Ed's empty seat.

Then someone was standing in front of the band, slashing a finger across their throat. "Medical emergency!" they shouted and waved for the guitar player to come quickly. Of course, the guitarist was another good friend of yours—and an emergency room doctor.

Another doctor had been listening to the band, and a third one was nearby hitting tennis balls with his wife while it was still light enough to play. In a way, the circumstances couldn't have been better. Moments after you collapsed, you had doctors and friends by your side. Plus, it happened at the club, which was such a big part of your life. You'd won a tennis match two days before, and your doubles partner told me it was the best she'd ever seen you play. People still talk about what a terrific social director you were at the club. You were always friendly to everyone and happy, effervescent. I think of you that way, too. You smiled and laughed. And danced.

I may have some of the details wrong. I talked with your friends who were there that night and tried to piece together what happened, though my questions were tentative. I wasn't sure how much to ask. I'd never had someone close to me die so suddenly. It was like being uprooted, shaken to the core, and if that's how I felt, I wondered what Mom and Dad were going through. The four of us had always shared a bond ourselves, and now you were gone and it didn't seem right. Actually, it didn't seem real.

When I talked with your friends, I thought of my years covering hard news and the times I posed delicate questions to the grief stricken. Now I was one of those grieving people and yet still playing the role of reporter. I was reporting and grieving at the same time and not doing a very good job of either. I suppose I was lost somewhere in between. As were you.

This is pure conjecture now, no reporting but just a feeling. I have a feeling that as you were lying on the ground at the party, with Ed holding your hand and calling your name and everyone circled around you, that you were both there and not there at the same time. I believe you were somewhere in between.

I bet during that critical moment no one paused, turned their head, and lifted their eyes to the dusky sky. They probably wouldn't have seen anything if they had, though I do believe you were there, floating over that frantic circle. I bet you said to yourself, *What in the world? What's going on?* Then you looked closely at the commotion below and saw yourself in the center lying prone and unresponsive, and I'm sure the realization was profound. I can see you smacking your chest with your hand the way you used to when you were surprised. *Oh, my gosh!* It was funny the way you'd say it with your open mouth and big eyes.

You may have told yourself, *Get up, Laura, c'mon,* but at some point very soon I think you realized you were not getting up—that you were between places, so to speak.

I wish I could ask you what that was like. Did you know you were looking at the end of your life and if so, *How did you feel?* There's that dreaded question. Callous reporters have been known to ask it of grieving parents who've lost their beautiful child.

But—how *did* you feel? Did you realize you'd never again hold Ed's hand or hug your children or see your friends, that you'd never hit another tennis ball, work out at your favorite fitness place, relax on the beach, watch movies, read books, talk to Mom and Dad or me? If you did know, were you traumatized by the revelation? Were you sad or at peace? Or did peace come later? I don't know the answers. All I have are the earthly details, and those seem terribly incomplete.

The EMTs arrived quickly and loaded you on a stretcher. Your heart stopped on the way to the hospital, but they were able to get it beating again.

Around that time, Mom and Dad had just sat down with their neighbors for a cocktail. The phone rang. "Laura's had some kind of seizure," Ed told Mom. There was alarm and concern but not panic. "Don't know," Ed said. "Not sure." The neighbors left right away, and Mom and Dad rushed to the hospital, thinking it was something temporary—or at least praying it was.

The guitar player-doctor had gone to the hospital, too, and studied your CT scan. The aneurysm was severe, he told me later. "A very bad bleed. One of the worst I've seen." He said it was probably something you always had, a weakness in one of the vessels deep inside your head. It could just as well have burst when you were a child, he explained. The miracle, he said, was that you lived as long as you had.

Still, you were only fifty-six. I was three years younger but had always thought I would go before you. I just assumed you'd live on and would be there to take care of Mom and Dad. All of you were in Virginia Beach, and I was almost four hours away in Raleigh. It never occurred to me you would die first and so soon.

All that time I spent as a reporter interviewing people, and yet I never interviewed *you*. I would have asked if you were afraid of dying and what you thought heaven was like. Knowing what I know now, I would have also asked how you were feeling before it happened and whether you had any inkling.

You were on life support when I arrived, and maybe you were above us in the hospital room, peering down at another circle that had formed around you. This time there was no commotion. We leaned against the bed rails and looked at you lying still and listened to the breathing machine hum and hiss. I think we knew we had a decision to make even before the doctor made it for us.

He wore green scrubs, spoke softly, and shifted his weight from one foot to the other. He said he had run a series of tests and explained each in detail more graphic than we wanted to hear. He told us there was no response.

"None?"

"I'm sorry, no. Nothing."

It was terrible for Mom and Dad. They'd seen you a few days before and now, just like that, you were gone, still breathing, but gone. I remember seeing the clothes you'd worn to the party gathered in a small pile on a chair near the window: a pair of baby blue shorts.

We each said our goodbyes. I touched your arm, swollen from the IV fluids. "I love you," I said for the first time and thought of my regrets, especially all my teasing when we were kids. But I didn't dwell on regret, or even on grief.

It was the miracles I mainly thought of, all the ones I'd been writing about. At one point, I actually did turn my head and gaze at the ceiling and smiled a little inside. You weren't floating up there, of course. By then, I sensed you were already at heaven's door. Or is it a gate or golden walkway? In any case, before the book I would not have smiled or thought of heaven with the same assuredness. But those people I interviewed were so convincing, humble and at peace, and none of them seemed to fear death at all. They made me a believer, not that I wasn't before, but a believer in a more real and tangible way. My reporting had done that. It had not provided me proof of heaven or God, but it had bridged that often-gaping space between truth and doubt. Between faith and air.

You never got to read the book. I'm not even sure I told you about it—one more regret. When I sat down to start it, I kept thinking about a particular creed, one that says nonfiction writers should grow as they're writing. When writers learn about themselves as the pages unfold, it keeps the story fresh and unpredictable. That's what I wanted for myself when I began, though I didn't really believe it would happen. Another little miracle is that it did.

Somewhere along the line I changed, which in turn compelled me to keep writing. I wanted to find out what would happen to me at the end—and the end was indeed unpredictable. I never saw it coming.

You died Sunday, October 4th, 2015.

I spent that week with Mom and Dad. You should have seen all the people who came to visit and the food they brought. Dad filled both freezers and still needed more room. We talked about you during those visits, but about other things, too. We laughed, and I kept thinking how much you would have enjoyed those good conversations.

There were difficult conversations as well. Ed came over one day and we worked on your obituary. He asked me if I'd like to speak at your funeral, and for hours I struggled with the words at Mom and Dad's kitchen table.

The worst was going to the funeral home one night and seeing you in the coffin. You wore a pink nightgown with short sleeves. The room was freezing, and I wished I'd brought a blanket for you. Ed, Lee, and Georgia brought scissors and took turns snipping strands of your hair, something of you they could keep. We were back at the funeral home the next night to receive friends. The line stretched all the way into the parking lot, and one by one people entered and shook hands with us. I asked too many questions and held up the line, but I wanted to get to know everyone. I was particularly struck by the short woman in the red dress. The dress seemed tight, and she kept pulling down the hem. She told me she knew you from Food Lion and that you always waited in line at her register even if another cashier was available. I thanked her for coming, and she smiled. She said she hadn't minded waiting in line, either.

The next day was beautiful, a Friday, and the church was full. People said they'd never seen a funeral so large or such an outpouring of love. During the service, Ed's band mates played a gentle medley, tearing up while they sang "Somewhere Over the Rainbow" and "It's a Wonderful World." You would have loved it, though I think you would have cried, too.

At the reception afterward, one of your friends told me about a letter you had written him years before. You remember him, I'm sure—the public figure who had done something wrong that threatened his career. At his lowest point, he discovered the note you slipped in his mailbox, and he told me how much your words of encouragement had meant.

I never knew you'd written that letter or waited at Food Lion or that you had so many dear and genuine friends. I didn't know you would die so young and how it would affect me. I think of you often and hear that little laugh of yours. I hear you say, *Hey, Scotty!* whenever you saw me, and *Catch ya' on the flip side!* whenever you left. It's still hard to believe you're gone, that everything you were is no more.

Your ashes are tucked in a columbarium behind the church. It's a pretty setting with lots of red brick and a handsome iron gate. Not all the ashes are sealed inside the wall. We kept some to spread at your favorite places: the beach and Mom and Dad's garden.

And what of the place you're in now? What is that place like exactly? That's what I set out to learn when I began this book, which at the end remains an unanswered question. I imagine it's a place beyond words.

And yet I do feel closer to God now and to understanding what heaven might be like. Slowly, the book became a gift in the way it changed me. The people on my miracle list changed me. They convinced me there is life beyond death, and not only that but gave me a glimpse of what that life is like. Once that revelation hit me, I began to think of my book differently. I wanted it to be my gift to God.

Regretfully—or thankfully—the gift is flawed because I'm still here. I can't truly know heaven, while you, Laura, have departed one wonderful world and joined another.

I think of you there in peace, embraced by God, enveloped in love—though I must admit, I do wonder what exactly you're up to up there. A silly question, I guess, but I have to ask. I'm a reporter—one still seeking answers.

Sometimes I look at the sky and say, "Hey, Laura!" I even say it out loud and imagine you calling back, *Hey, Scotty!* One day I hope I'll see you up there—though, sorry, I do hope it's not for a while yet. I laugh a little, confident you're happy and in a good place. A part of me cries some, too.

So, Laura, that's it. I've finished my miracle list, glad that I have, though not altogether satisfied. A reporter rarely is—and in this case, neither is a brother. I seem to always be searching. And I suppose a good Christian is, too—for greater faith and a closer relationship with God.

You, Laura, are already there, and I'm not sure if I'm sad or envious—both, I guess. I just can't believe you're gone, no longer on this earth, and it's made me think.

I think what I've learned is that believing is what it's all about. I believed the people on my miracle list, and I believe you are in heaven—I just wish I knew more about it. I trust one day I will.

One day, I pray, I'll catch ya' on the flip side.

Love,
Scotty

ABOUT THE AUTHOR

SCOTT MASON is a broadcast journalist with more than thirty years of television experience. He has won dozens of awards for documentaries, writing, and feature reporting, including three National Edward R. Murrow awards and twenty regional Emmys. The Electronic News Association of the Carolinas has twice named him the North Carolina Television Reporter of the Year.

Today, Scott is known as the Tar Heel Traveler. His Monday through Thursday feature series on WRAL takes viewers along the back roads of North Carolina where he meets memorable characters, finds out-of-the-way places, and unearths fascinating historical footnotes.

Scott has also published two books about his television adventures: *Tar Heel Traveler: Journeys across North Carolina* (2010) and *Tar Heel Traveler Eats: Food Journeys across North Carolina* (2014)—both through Rowman and Littlefield Press.

Scott graduated in 1984 from Washington and Lee University in Lexington, Virginia, where he majored in Journalism and Communications. He earned his MFA degree in creative writing from Queens University of Charlotte in 2015.

Scott lives in Raleigh with his wife Nina, daughters Lane and Genie, and son Scout.

Follow Scott and his writing at thetarheeltraveler.com.

MORE TITLES BY SCOTT MASON

Tar Heel Traveler: Journeys across North Carolina

Tar Heel Traveler Eats: Food Journeys across North Carolina

If you liked

FAITH AND AIR

you might also enjoy these titles from
Light Messages Publishing & Torchflame Books

Following the Red Bird: First Steps into a Life of Faith
Kate H. Rademacher

Raised by Strangers
Brooke Lynn

From Fortress to Freedom
Deborah L.W. Roszel

Jonah: A Tale of Mercy
Jimmy Long